CONTENTS

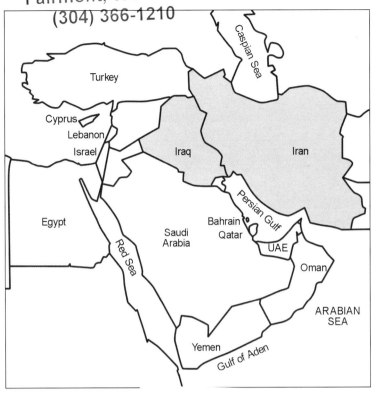

Helion & Company Limited
26 Willow Road
Solihull
West Midlands
B91 1UE
England
Tel. 0121 705 3393
Fax 0121 711 4075
email: info@helion.co.uk
website: www.helion.co.uk

Text © E.R. Hooton, Tom Cooper and Farzin Nadimi 2018
Colour profiles © Tom Cooper and Peter Penev 2018
Maps George Anderson © Helion & Company Limited 2018
Photographs © as individually credited

Designed & typeset by Farr out Publications, Wokingham, Berkshire
Cover design by Paul Hewitt, Battlefield Design (www.battlefield-design.co.uk)
Printed by Henry Ling Limited, Dorchester, Dorset

ISBN 978-1-911512-45-5

British Library Cataloguing-in-Publication Data.
A catalogue record for this book is available from the British Library.

For details of other military history titles published by Helion & Company Limited contact the above address, or visit our website: http://www.helion.co.uk. We always welcome receiving book proposals from prospective authors.

Acknowledgments

We would like to thank Dr Kevin W.Woods, one of the leading researchers in the Iran-Iraq War, for his extremely useful advice in following certain lines of research; to Major General Aladdin Hussein Makki Khamas for his patient responses and advices to many querries; and to Colonel Pesach Malovany, one of the leading non-Arab authorities on the Iraqi Army, for his assistance and advice. Finally, we would like to express our gratitude to a number of Iranian veterans of this war who helped by providing translated excerpts from numerous books published in Farsi, as well as with personal recollections and photographs – all on condition of anonymity.

Note

In order to simplify the use of this book, all names, locations and geographic designations are as provided in The Times World Atlas, or other traditionally accepted major sources of reference, as of the time of described events. Similarly, Arabic names are romanised and transcripted rather than transliterated. For example: the definite article al- before words starting with 'sun letters' is given as pronounced instead of simply as al- (which is the usual practice for non-Arabic speakers in most English-language literature and media).

Glossary and abbreviations

AFV	Armoured Fighting Vehicle
Arm	Armoured
Arty	Artillery
ATGM	anti-tank guided missile
Bde	Brigade
Cdo	Commando
CFOHQ	Central Forward Operational Headquarters (Iranian)
CIA	Central Intelligence Agency (USA)
COMINT	Communications intelligence
CSG/GSG	Combat Support/General Support Groups (IRIAA formations)
Div	Division
ETOH	East of Tigris Operations Headquarters (Iraqi)
FEBA	Forward Edge of Battle Area
'Gainful' ASCC	Codename for 2K12 Kub Cube surface-to air missile also designated SA-6
Gd	Republican Guards (Iraqi)
GHQ	General Headquarters
GMID	General Military Intelligence Directorate (Iraqi) or Mudiriyyat al-Istikhabarat al-Askariyya al-Amma.
GSD	Iraqi Security Agency (Mudiriyat al-Amn al-Ameh)
IFV	Infantry fighting vehicle
IrAAC	Iraqi Army Aviation Corps
IrAF	Iraqi Air Force
IRIA	Islamic Republic of Iran Army
IRIAA	Islamic Republic of Iran Army Aviation
IRIAF	Islamic Republic of Iran Air Force
MANPADS	Man-Portable Air Defence System. Light surface-to-air missile system which can be carried and deployed in combat by a single soldier
MBT	Main Battle Tank
Mech	Mechanised
MeK	Mujahideen e-Khalq. (Iranian armed opposition, based in Iraq)
MLRS	Multiple Launch Rocket System
NFOHQ	Northern Forward Operational Headquarters (Iranian)
Pasdaran	Iranian Revolutionary Guards Corps. Members are Pasdaran
RGWHQ	Ramadan Guerrilla Warfare Headquarters (Iran)

CHAPTER 1
THE OPENING OPERATIONS

Background

While the Southern Front was the decisive theatre of the Iran-Iraq War, its Northern and Central Fronts attracted relatively little attention.

The warfare in this part of the world was always dictated by the local terrain. In contrast to the flat battlefields of the south, the terrain stretching north from the Hawizah Marshes is characterized by ridges that gradually merge into the Zagros Mountains (Kuhha-ye Zagros), some of which climb to more than 2,000 metres above sea level. The Northern Front ran from the tri-border area between Iran, Iraq, and Turkey, with fighting touching the Iraqi provinces of Arbil, as-Sulaymaniyah, Diyala, and northern Dahuk, and the Iranian provinces of Azerbayejan-e-Gharabi, Kordestan, Kermanshah, and northern Ilam. There are two major lakes in this area: Lake Dukan (Buhayrat Dukan), 100 kilometres north-west of the town of Sulaymaniyah, and the Lake Darband-i-Khan (Buhayrat Darband-i-Khan), about 20 kilometres south-west of it.

The Central Front touched the Iraqi provinces of Diyala, Wasit and Maysan, and the Iranian provinces of southern Ilam and northern Khuzestan. Here the elevations are lower, averaging 500-2,000 metres above sea level. Indeed, on the Iraqi side of the foothills they drop into terrain that features sand dunes and descends to the northern tip of the Hawizah Marshes in al-Amarah area. Eastern Diyala province is characterized by extensive marshes fed by numerous tributaries of the Tigris descending from the Zagrous Mountains – including Hawr Suwayqiyah in the south – that stretch for some 150 by 110 kilometres. To the east of the marshes is a narrow strip of ground, some 10-13 kilometres wide and averaging about 250-400 metres above sea level. This runs parallel to the border with Iran to a point just south of the Mehran salient. Eastern Wasit and Maysan consist of undulating terrain broken by low hills and criss-crossed by waterways. This is an area suitable for manoeuvring- and mechanized warfare, although high ground on the Iranian side tends to restrict movement eastwards.

Towering Zagros mountains in western Iran. (Mark Lepko Collection)

Dukan Lake, in north-eastern Iraq. (Mark Lepko Collection)

The Zagroz Mountains tower like a big curtain on the western side of the Mesopotamian plains. (Mark Lepko Collection)

The Fronts' Infrastructure

The terrain restricts cross-border commercial transport to a handful of roads, while movement into Iran is restricted to a limited number of passes through the mountains. Furthermore, mountainous terrain means that communications are often disrupted by weather; rains cause flooding and landslides, while snow can block roads for weeks. Due to the lack of interest in cross-border connections, most of the road networks constructed during the 1950s and 1960s run parallel to the frontier, following different valleys. Nevertheless, roads remain essential due to the scarcity of railways, most of which are either single-track, or have narrow gauge lines, limiting their capacity.

During the reign of the Shah Mohammed Reza Pahlavi, Iran built a number of major military installations to control border crossings – such as Orumiyeh, Sanandaj (also known as Sinnah), and Khermanshah (renamed Bakhtaran in December 1981 but later reverting to its original name). Further north is a main road linking Arbil (or Erbil), Shaqlawah, Rawandiz (or Rawanduz), to Piranshahr, Urumia (or Orumiyeh), while Sulaymaniyeh is connected to Kirkuk via a highwawy that continues in the form of a secondary road eastwards towards Penjwin, and then to Marivan (or Dezh Shapur). Closer to the border with Iran, only one secondary road connects the eastern shore of Lake Darband-i-Khan with Halabja, from where a few tracks cross the frontier to Nowsud. On the southern side, Sulaymaniyeh is connected with the Baghdad-Kirkuk and Babgdad-Baquba highways via a network of secondary roads. The highway connecting Baghdad with Basra runs along the Tirgris through al-Kut, al-Amarah and al-Qurnah.

In the area along the central sector of the border between Iran and Iraq, Diyala is connected to Baghdad by a main road that branches eastwards at Khanaqin. One link leads to Qasr-e Shirin and Sar-e-Pol-e-Zohab before becoming a secondary road to Eslamabad-e Gharb. In between major roads there are a significant number of gravelled, or simply beaten-earth, roads, some of these extending beyond the borders. Towns like Badrah (northern Wasit), and at-Tib (also 'Teeb'; in central Maysan) are crossroads for the road networks on the Iraqi side, while inside Iran Mehran and Musiyan are their offshoots.

Deeper behind the border, on the Iranian side, the road network is much poorer. There is only one main road running from Suma to Eslam Abd-e-Gharb, then Ilam, Mehran, and Dehloran. This splits near Musyan, with one branch going east to Dezful and the other following the frontier through Fakkeh (or Fakke or Fuka) to Bostan, then Susangerd, and Ahwaz.

Population

While terrain was one factor affecting military operations, another one – especially along the northernmost part of the border between Iran and Iraq – was the population. Most numerous in this part of the world are Kurds: an ethnic group that is culturally, historically, and linguistically classified as belonging to the Iranian peoples, but the majority of whom are Sunni Moslems.

Often described as, 'the largest ethnic group without a state', the Kurds are split into numerous tribes and clans and speek dozens of different dialects, some of which are akin to foreign languages. With Kurds being successfully integrated (though not assimilated) into the Ottoman Empire, their nationalism emerged only during WWI, when Young Turks launched a large-scale deporation of Kurds. The Treaty of Sévres promised at least autonomy, if not outright independence for Kurds, and a Kingdom of Kurdistan was declared in Iraq from 1922 until 1924. However, traditional disunity between major Kurdish tribes, intensive efforts of Kemal Atatürk, and complaints by numerous other minorities living in the same area – including Arabs, Christians and Yezidis – all conspired to prevent the establishment of a viable state. Multiple Kurdish uprisings which erupted over the following decades were bloodily supressed, first by the British, then by the Iraqis. In the 1970s, Kurdish nationalism led to several insurgencies with their leaders openly challenging traditional feudal authorities. Divisions between them ensured that Baghdad and Tehran always had a strong foundation of support within 'Kurdish' territories.

In 1974 the Kurdish Democratic Party (Partiya Demokrat a Kurdistane; KDP) under Mullah Mustafa Barzani and his sons Idris and Masoud, launched an uprising.[1] The KDP was actually a conservative organization, based upon the tribal system and emphasizing personal leadership. Tehran provided clandestine, even if large-scale military support for this rebellion, openly threatening both Iraqi national unity and the economy. Although initially highly successful, this insurgency was crushed by the Iraqi military in the aftermath of the Iranian withdrawal following the Algiers Treaty of 1975. Afterwards, Iraqi authorities dispersed up to 200,000 Kurds into resettlement camps scattered throughout the country. The Barzani family went into exile to re-organise, Mustafa dying in 1979 in the United States, while many of their followers fled to Iran. In

Mustafa Barzani as seen during the uprising of 1974-1975. (Mark Lepko Collection)

Jalal Talabani (right) at the HQ of his PUK. (Mark Lepko Collection)

July 1979 the Barzani brothers, seeing an opportunity to renew their armed struggle, moved to Iran which began supporting the PDK the following year.[2]

Meanwhile, a new Kurdish leader appeared in the form of Jalal Talabani, a moderniser who sought to establish a modern democracy based upon socialist ideas. Forced into exile in Iran by Barzani's forces in 1964, Talabani played little part in the 1974-1975 revolt, but in May of the latter year established a new group in Damascus, named the Patriotic Union of Kurdistan (Yekêtiy Niştîmaniy Kurdistan; PUK), as an umbrella organization for like-minded Kurds to offer a modern alternative to the Barzani's vision. The resulting division between the KDP and the PUK was as much as political as it was ethnic: KDP-supporters spoke the Kurmanji dialect, while those of the PUK spoke the Sorani dialect. When Talabani's men pushed into KDP's heartland of Arbil and Dahuk, in 1976-1977, fierce clashes erupted, causing a deep rift within the entire Kurdish nation. The PUK failed to dislodge the KDP, but over the following years managed to steadily extend its influence into Arbil, becoming the primary resistance force against Iraqi authorities.

Events of 1979

The Iranian-supported KDP revolt of 1974-1975 polarised not only the Kurds, but the entire Iraqi society too. Many Iraqi Shi'a were sympathetic, to a degree, and decades later, after the fall of the regime of Saddam Hussein at-Tikriti (Saddam), – the Shi'a-dominated government in Baghdad granted full autonomy to the northern regions.

In the meantime, Saddam – despite helping negotiate the Algiers Treaty and granting autonomy to the Kurds – tended to declare them as 'saboteurs', and considered them a threat to Iraq's unity.[3] He received considerable support for his actions against the Kurds from different parties within Iraq, a British journalist later noted:

'Even anti-government exiles wax indignant at the Kurds'

treacherous behaviour during the Gulf war.'[4]

Therefore, while the Algiers Treaty had helped Iraq crush the revolt, it remained a thorn in Saddam's side, a sign of national weakness in comparison to Iran, and one in which he had been intimately involved. Consequently, he was determined to reverse it as soon as possible. A suitable opportunity offered itself in 1979, when the revolution in Iran toppled the Shah Reza Pahlavi, to be replaced by a cleric-led administration under Ayatollah Ruhollah al-Musavi al-Khomeini (Khomeini). The post-revolutionary chaos, power struggles, a counter-coup attempt and massive purges of the military left Iran in such chaos that it appeared unable to defend itself. Indeed, only two months after the Shah was forced to leave Iran, Kurdish nationalists – who wholeheartedly supported the revolution to that point – were denied the seats in the newly-established Assembly of Experts in Tehran. As a result the Democratic Party of Iranian Kurdistan (KDPI), and the leftist Revolutionary Organization of Kurdish Toilers (Komala) launched an uprising against the Iranian revolutionary government and by late April, sectarian fighting broke out between Kurdish and Azeri factions, resulting in hundreds of casualties.

As the violence spread, many Kurdish conscripts from the regional military garrisons brought the strength of the KDPI's insurgency to about 30,000 fighters, colloquially known as Peshmerga (Death Defiers). The insurgency brought most of Kordistan and Gharei under control, leaving Tehran controlling only the major population centres, and even these had to be supplied from the air. That the uprising had popular support became obvious in March 1979, when the traiditional Kurdish capital of Mahabad, in Gharei, was taken by combined forces of Abdu Rahman Ghassemlou, the KDPI's leader, and the local Kurdish Sunni religious leader, Sheikh Ezzadin Husseini.[5]

The two locally based units of the Islamic Republic of Iran Army (IRIA) – the Urumia-based 64th Infantry Division and Sanandaj-based 28th Infantry Division – tried to contain the threat, but their ranks had been drained by post-revolutionary purges. Furthermore, the clerics placed greater faith in the emerging Islamic Revolutionary Guards Corps (IRGC, also Sepah-e Pasdaran-e Enghelab-e Eslami, or Pasdaran). The Pasdaran were initially too fragmented to provide effective resistence, and even by the end of 1979 still operated only in platoons and companies of up to about 80 men. They reacted by deploying a large force, but this was ambushed while marching upon the Kurdish-held town of Paveh, and suffered grievous casualties.

Undaunted, the new government of the Islamic Republic of Iran (IRI) declared a 'Jihad' (holy war) and issued a fatwa (religious edict), declaring the Iranian Kurds and their key leaders 'enemies of the state'. Fearing Iraqi support for the Kurds, and finding out that Ghassemlou had been joined by Talebani's PUK operating from the Iraqi province of Suleymaniyah, Tehran even recalled military officers who had received extensive training in counter-insurgency (COIN) operations from US advisors in the 1960s and 1970s. In August 1979, the Iranian military – supported by McDonnell Douglas F-4E Phantom II fighter-bombers from the Tactical Fighter Base 3 (TFB.3) of the Islamic Republic of Iran Air Force (IRIAF), near Hamedan, Bell AH-1J Cobra, and Bell 214A Esfahan helicopters of the Islamic Republic of Iran Army Air Corps (IRIAA) – was unleashed upon the Kurdish-held town of Mahabad. In the course of a three-day long siege the Kurds were soundly defeated.

Despite the failure to secure Mahabad, by the end of the year the KDPI still controlled territory up to 75 kilometres east of their Gharbi Mountains heartland while Husseini's enclave extended 50 kilometres from the Iraqi border.[6]

The more crises and internal and external threats Iran faced in 1979 and 1980, the more opportunity the local Shi'a clergy found to recruit the population. Ultimately, this enabled the 'Mullahs' to secure their rule over the entire country – but also to become influential in regards of military-related affairs. (Albert Grandolini Collection)

A group of volunteers of the future Islamic Revolutionary Guards Corps, listening to the lecture of their preacher. (Albert Grandolini Collection)

The IRGC crushed the Kurdish uprising in north-western Iran in blood, often summarily executing captured enemy fighters, as well as any activists, or suspects it could lay its hands upon. (Mark Lepko Collection)

Meanwhile, Saddam began claiming that Iran had failed to honour the Algiers Treaty and – starting in May 1980 – began deploying troops to 'liberate' territory claimed by Iraq, causing a series of low-intensity clashes along much of the border. The Iranian response was weak and confused, but in early June 1980, the Iraqi Military Intelligence (GMID) reported large concentrations of the KDP in the Sardash area. Correspondingly, No. 1 Squadron of the Iraqi Air Force (IrAF), based at al-Hurrya Air Base (AB) near Kirkuk was ordered to deploy eight Sukhoi Su-20 fighter-bombers for a strike against one of the Kurdish bases inside Iran. This attack was flown on 4 June 1980, and caused not only considerable losses to the Kurds, but also an uproar from Tehran. It was also a signal for both sides to resort to use of air power to support their respective interests and ground forces in what became a series of small-scale operations along the border.

On 7 September 1980, the 16th Armoured Brigade of the 6th Armoured Division, Iraqi Army, seized the plateau of Zayn al-Qaws. Three days later, Brigadier-General Hisham Sabah al-Fakhri's 10th Armoued Division took the Saif Sa'ad enclave. Meanwhile, Iran continued sliding ever deeper into chaos, and thus Saddam decided to launch an invasion of the country, code-named Qadisiyya II, with the aim of seizing additional territory and helping overthrow Khomeni, or at least to enforce a re-negotiation of the Algiers Treaty from a favourable position.[7]

Iraq invades

While Saddam's primary objectives were within the province of Khuzestan, in south-western Iran, he was determined to secure key areas in the northern mountains and the foothills of the Zagros Mountains too. For this purpose, the Iraqi Army deployed its I Corps (commanded by Lieutenant-General Mohammed Fathi Amin) and II Corps (Lieutenant-General Abadallah Abd al-Latif al-Hudaythi) (for a detailed order of battle of these and other involved forces, see Table 1). Saddam did consider assisting the rebellion of dissident Iranian Kurds, but feared this might encourage Iraqi Kurds to launch their own uprising, and thus ordered Amin to focus upon counter-insurgency (COIN) operations. Indeed, the I Corps even had to transfer some of its troops under the command of the II Corps. This left it with its 11th Infantry Division on the defensive in the north, while the 7th Mountain Division advanced along the Penjwin-Marivan and Halabja-Nosud roads, with the aim of 'retaking' areas occupied by the Iranians in 1975. Latif's units bore the brunt of the cross-border operations. The emphasis of these was an attack on Qasr-e Shirin by the 8th Infantry and 6th Armoured Divisions, while the 4th Mountain and 12th Armoured Divisions were to take Naft Shahr and Summar, respectively, and threaten Kermanshah. The 2nd Infantry Division (reinforced by 37th Armoured Brigade from the 10th Armoured Division) was to secure the Mehran Salient, and threaten Ilam, while the remainder of the 10th Armoured Division was sent to reinforce the III Corps in Khuzestan.[8]

Hindered by complete chaos in their state and the military, and the Kurdish uprising in the north, the Iranians were slow to react. Furthermore, they also misinterpreted Iraqi attacks upon their

A still from a video, showing Iraqi T-55s lining-up prior to the start of another advance into Iran in late September 1980. (Tom Cooper Collection)

During the opening Iraqi strike of the war, a formation of MiG-21bis from No. 47 Squadron bombed the Iranian Army base in Orumiyeh. The aircraft flown by Lt Ra'ad Hamid was blown up by premature detonation of its bombs and the pilot killed. (Tom Cooper Collection)

border posts as an Iraqi attempt to support the Kurds in a similar fashion to what the Shah did in Iraq in 1974-1975.

Nominally, the IRIA had three divisions and two brigades facing what became the northern and central fronts. However, the Urumia-based 64th Infantry Division, and Sanandaj-based 28th Infanrtry Division were in no condition to deploy and initially remained unengaged. Latif thus faced the Kermanshah-based 81st Armoured Division, reinforced by the 40th (Srab) and 84th (Khorramabad) Independent Infantry Brigades. Eventually, the 2nd Brigade of the Ahwaz-based 92nd Armoured Division was re-deployed to the central front lines at a later stage.

All the units were severely under strength due to neglect and purges, even though augumented by the Border Guards, Gendarmerie, Police, civilian volunteers and Pasdaran. Their initial resistance was weak apart from the odd Border Guard post, some of whose garrisons fought to the death. Generally, there were too few Irnaian troops near the frontier, while the IRIA's battalions were very slow to deploy westwards.[9]

As in Khuzestan it thus fell upon Iranian air power to prove as the greatest obstacle to the Iraqi progress. The IRIAA operated an entire Combat Support Group – totaling about 24 each of AH-1Js, Bell 214s, and a company of Boeing CH-47 Chinook transport helicopters – deployed at Kermanshah. Indeed, the first IRIA reinforcements to the border were deployed with the help of helicopters on 14 September 1980. Immediately afterwards, Iran's president, Abol Hassan Bani-Sadr, ordered a ceasefire in the Kurdish region, to allow his troops to concentrate on the Iraqi aggression. Ironically, the Revolutionary Guards ignored his order and continued fighting Kurds, so that only a weak screen of the IRIA's ground troops protected the border. Bani-Sadr also offered

the KDPI a cease-fire, so he could concentrate on the west.[10]

Khomeini eventually found a solution in offering the KDP a deal: its 800 Peshmerga still active in Iraq, and about 5,000 men under arms in Iran, should fight the KDPI and the PUK, in exchange for money and arms. Full repercussions of this decision were to become obvious only years later.

The IRIAF was present foremost in the form of Northrop F-5E Tiger II fighters from the TFB.2 (Tabriz) and F-4E Phantom IIs from TFB.3. Operating with the support of Forward Air Controllers (FACs) and Direct Air Support Centres (DASCs) assigned to army units and major headquarters, respectivelly, this proved highly effective in knocking out dozens of Iraqi vehicles. Indeed, their activity during the weeks before the war, and then the first weeks after the Iraqi invasion grew to a degree where the Iraqis were forced to re-deploy batteries of SA-6 Gainful surface-to-air missiles (SAM) from Baghdad to the vicinity of the border in order to bolster their air defences. However, while the air power proved effective in destroying much of the Iraqi oil industry, and thus blocking fuel supplies for the front, left on its own it was insufficient to prevent the invaders from establishing good blocking positions from which they could beat off spasmodic and uncoordinated Iranian attacks.[11]

Table 1: Order of Battle for Iraqi Invasion of Iran, Northern & Central Fronts, September 1980

Corps	Division	Brigades
Iraq		
I Corps	2nd Mountain Division	3 brigades
	4th Mountain Division	3 brigades
	7th Mountain Division	3 brigades
	8th Infantry Division	4 brigades
	11th Infantry Division	4 brigades
	12th Armoured Division	4 brigades
	31st Special Forces Brigade	
	32nd Special Forces Brigade	
II Corps	3rd Armoured Division	4 brigades
	6th Armoured Division	4 brigades
	10th Armoured Division	4 brigades
	31st Special Forces Brigade	
Iran		
	29th Infantry Division (Sanandaj)	4 brigades (-)
	64th Infantry Division (Urumia)	4 brigades (-)
	81st Armoured Division (Kermanshah)	4 brigades (-)
	40th Independent Infantry Brigade (Sarab)	
	84th Independent Infantry Brigade (Khorramabad)	
	2nd Brigade	from 92nd Armoured Division

Qasr-e Shirin Sector

Dominating a prominent salient into Iraq, Qasr-e Shirin was a town about 20 kilometres from the border in between fertile, undulating plains in the west, and the Zagros Mountains in the east: overall

A group of Iranian Army soldiers with the ejection seat of Ra'ad Hamid's MiG-21bis. (Tom Cooper Collection)

Another early loss of the Iraqi Air Force over the central front was this Su-22, claimed shot down on 24 September 1980, in the Marivan area. (Tom Cooper Collection)

The Iranian Army had only around 11,000 troops deployed along the central and northern sectors of the front lines at the start of the war. However, the Iraqi invasion prompted dozens of thousands of Iranians to volunteer for military service. (Albert Grandolini Collection)

good tank country, broken by relatively few low hills and ravines. Most of the population fled in the days before the Iraqi invasion, while the most important position was the Baytaq Pass, a narrow defile through which ran the road to Kermanshah.

Commandos of the 32nd Special Forces Brigade cleared the way for the 6th Armoured Division and 8th Infantry Division during the night from 22 to 23 September 1980, by securing a bridge near Emam Hassan and key peaks around Sar-e Pol-e Zahab. The 25th Mechanized Brigade (6th Armoured Division) then isolated Qasr-e Shirin from the north-east, while the 30th Armoured Brigade pushed eastwards on Sar-e Pol-e Zahab. As the Iraqis progressed deeper into Iran they used tactics based on strong artillery support used to ease the progress of the infantry. This became ever more important as the IRIA began deploying its highly effective artillery groups. Worse still the Kurds, whom Baghdad believed would regard the Iraqis as liberators now began harassing their advance.

Nevertheless, the two Iraqi brigades pushed down the road before running into elements of an IRIAF mechanized infantry platoon and two companies with about 25 main battle tanks (MBTs). These delayed them for two days, and Qasr-e Shirin thus fell only on 27 September 1980.[12]

Assault on Gilan-e Gharb

The only major IRIA formation in this part of Iran – 81st Armoured Division – took two days to bring at least its 1st Brigade into operational order. This was deployed westwards from Kermanshah. Its 3rd Brigade moved out of its barracks on the next day and then quickly stopped the advance of 25th Mechanized Brigade on Sar-e Pol-e Zahab. Similarly, a weak battalion group was enough to stop the first Iraqi attack on Gilan-e Gharb.

The Iraqi caution in these operations was outright remarkable, considering their superiority in heavy weaponry. According to US intelligence assessments, the Iraqi Army had 282 MBTs against 42 Iranian as of mid-October 1980, and its 183 artillery pieces were

M60A1 MBTs and an AH-1J Cobra attack helicopter of the Iranian Army as seen in a forward base in the central sector of the Iran-Iraq War in late 1980. (Tom Cooper Collection)

facing some 65 Iranian. However, the Iraqis were critically short on infantry: after their 30th Armoured Brigade suffered heavy losses – mostly to nocturnal Iranian counterattacks – it had to be reinforced by two battalions of 3rd Infantry Brigade.[13] Meanwhile, 8th Infantry Division pushed on Gilan-e Gharb, with the 22nd Infantry Brigade advancing from the south towards Kojar Pass, and the 3rd Infantry Brigade on the Sisar Heights in the north. However, these forces proved inadequate: the need to protect their lines-of-communication (LOCs) meant the two Iraqi brigades were unable to take the town.

Further south, Brigadier-General Muhammad Ismail al-Weis led his 12th Armoured Division towards Sumar. His unit was a recently-converted infantry formation, and Weis had to relinquish his 37th Armoured Brigade to the 2nd Infantry Division. However, in turn he received 10th Armoured Brigade (Colonel Mahmud Shukr Shahin) from the General Headquarters (GHQ). Even then, his advance was led by 46th Mechanized Brigade – which, after colliding with elements of 2nd Brigade of the 81st Armoured Division at Nafte-Shah – required two days of bitter fighting to to punch through towards Gilan-e Gharb. Meanwhile, Shahin's brigade supported 4th Mountain Division's advance on Sumar, which was reached by the morning of 24 September, while 5th Mountain Brigade (Lieutenant-Colonel Sultan Hashim Ahmad) cleared the way for Shukr Shain by advancing over the Haran Plateau, then suppporing the capture of Sumar, before pushing on Gilan-e Gharb.

This combination of five brigades – further reinforced by the 18th and 29th Infantry Brigades – eventually managed to break through and briefly took Gilan-e Gharb on 28 September. However, they were forced out in a matter of few hours.[14]

The primary reason for this failure was the habit of Iraqi drivers of bunching their vehicles like a flock of sheep whenever under fire, rather than dispersing them. Despite losing their top pilot – Major-General Mansour Vatanpour, who was shot down and killed – attack helicopters of the IRIAA thus found a 'target rich environment' and exploited the opportunity to score dozens of kills.[15]

This bought the time for 81st Armoured Division IRIA to start implementing its defensive plan "Abuzar" (one of Prophet Mohammed's companions, Hazrat Abu Zar Ghaffari), and deploy its forces into delaying operations along a 600 kilometre wide frontline. Reinforced by Border Guards, Gendarmerie, Pasdaran and Kurdish tribesmen, the Iranian Army then launched increasingly stronger counter-attacks while divisional artillery harassed the invader joined by fierce fixed-wing and rotary-wing air support. Eventually, the Iraqis were not only stopped, but also by mid-December 1980 found themselves exposed to the first Iranian counter-offensive – the primary benefit of which was to keep the enemy in their positions until snow ended operations in that year.[16]

Mehran Sector

An important Iraqi objective was the town of Mehran, with a population of about 75,000. This occupies a pincer-like salient into Iraqi territory, pointing in direction of Baghdad, some 150 kilometres to the west. Furthermore, its occupation was to protect the fertile fields of Diyala Province and al-Kut (Kut al-Imara), with their citrus groves and orchards, some 75 kilometres away, and result in the capture of the Kunjan Dam on the River Galal Badra.

Mehran was defended by a weak battalion battlegroup of 1st Brigade 81st Armoured Division, which faced overwhelming odds – in the form of Brigadier-General Hazim Sulayman al-Barhawi's 2nd Infantry Division. Barhavi deployed his 4th Infantry Brigade and elements of 33rd Special Forces Brigade north of Mehran towards Konjam Cham Pass, and captured the Dam on 24 September 1980. His main attack – involing 36th Infantry and 37th Armorued Brigades – came along the main road and was held for two hours

Saddam and King Hussein of Jordan inspecting tanks (including a M60A1 MBT) captured early during the Iraqi invasion of Iran. (Tom Cooper Collection)

The first Iraqi soldier taken prisoner of war by the Iranians in the Ilam area, in late September 1980. (via Ali Tobchi)

A still from a video showing one of Iraqi T-62s involved in advance on Dezful, in late September and early October 1980. (Tom Cooper Collection)

An SA.342 Gazelle attack helicopter of the Iraqi Army Air Corps underway low over the frontlines west of Dezful in October 1980. (via Ali Tobchi)

at a berm-covered anti-armour ditch. Nevertheless, he entered the town on the morning of 24 September.

As the defenders withdrew eastwards, the Iraqis followed into a river-crossed plain with numerous ridges and defiles, which were easy to defend. This slowed the invader's advance to a crawl, with little artillery or air support. The Iraqi problems were increased by their own commando attack on the Galal Badra irrigation dam, which flooded much of the area.[17] Unsurprisingly, 2nd Infantry Brigade was still three kilometers from Ilam by the end of September and had no prospect of proceeding – especially once the Iranians solidified their positions.[18]

In early October, 8th Infantry Division (including 3rd, 22nd, and 23rd Infantry Brigades) took over responsibility for the Qasr-e Shirin sector, while the 2nd Infantry and 4th Mountain Divisions did the same in the south. Latif then ordered the demolition of buildings in Qasr-e Shirin, Gilan-e Ghab and Sumar, to use their timber and girders to build fortifications and thus tighten the grip. All of his positions were to receive overhead protection, and were dispersed to reduce the impact of artillery and air strikes. Furthermore, his units withdrew as many of their non-combat elements as possible to reduce the strain on supplies. Even then, the Iraqis in the Mehran area were clearly overstretched, and by the end of 1980 had to be reinforced by a battalion-sized battlegroup from 12th Armoured Division.[19]

Battle for Dezful

On Latif's right Major General Adnan Kadum's III Corps operations into the southern part of Iran's Ilam Province and the northern part of Khuzestan – centred around Major-General Abdul Hamid at-Tikriti's 1st Mechanized Division (including 1st and 27th Mechanised, and 34th Armoured Brigades) – aimed to complete control of the Iranian frontier road system. This push did pose a threat to Dezful too, although the Iraqis insist they never planned to capture the city.

On 20 September 1980, Saddam replaced Kadum with Lieutenant-General Ismael Tayeh an-Niami, and then reinforced III Corps with Major-General Sabah al-Fakhri's 10th Armoured Division (including 17th and 42nd Armoured, and 24th Mechanized Brigades).[20] Sabah used 24th Mechanised Brigade to isolate the battlefield from the north by striking from Tib, while 17th Armoured Brigade – followed by 42nd and supported by 24 artillery batteries – took Musiyan and then attacked Eyn Kush. The local IRIA garrison consisted of 2nd Brigade from the 92nd Armoured Division, but this had only five serviceable MBTs and three M113 APCs with TOW launchers. Although anti-armour missiles took a

Despite success, the Battle of Dezful proved costly for the IRIAF's TFB.4: at least four of its F-5Es – including the example shown here (presented to foreign journalists as 'an Iraqi') – were shot down by Iraqi ground defences. (Albert Grandolini Collection)

heavy toll of Iraqi tanks, Dasht Abbas fell on 26 September, enabling invaders to push on to Dezful. Upon reaching the Khark River they found two out of three bridges demolished, while the surviving construction was only suitable for pedestrian traffic. Relentless air strikes by F-5Es from the nearby TFB.4 – including extensive use

F-5Es from the Tactical Fighter Base 4 (TFB.4) played a crucial role in the defence of Dezful and their home base. During 15 days of the Battle for Dezful, between 27 September and 11 October 1980, they flew 324 attack sorties, and claimed the destruction of 170 Iraqi tanks and other armoured vehicles, forcing invaders into a retreat. (Tom Cooper Collection)

of CBUs – then caused such losses that the Iraqi commanders soon found themselves lacking troops and equipment to cross the river. The Iranians are known to have flown 324 sorties against this area within a fortnight, and to have lost seven aircraft to air defences. This campaign proved at least sufficient to discourage any kind of Iraqi ambitions with regards to Dezful. Instead, the III Corps limited its activities in this area to shelling. Even a battery of LUNA-M (FROG-7) rockets was deployed for this purpose. At least six of its weapons were fired, causing around 470 casualties.

After regrouping, the Iraqis attacked Dehloran on 13 October; although managing to enter the town they were quickly driven out. Indeed, between 14 and 16 October, a brigade-sized element of 92nd Armoured Division launched a series of counter-attacks that struck the 10th Armoured Division's left flank. The 42nd Armoured and 24th Mechanized Brigades counterattacked and recovered the lost ground, claiming the capture of 136 armoured vehicles – including 84 MBTs – in the process. During this fighting Iran's Major General Muhammad Reza Ziaie was killed.

The Dezful sector then became quiet. The IRIA deployed its 21st Division (created from two former Imperial Guard divisions) to reinforce defences, together with a battalion of M60 MBTs from the 77th Infantry Division, and a battalion of Marines. However, the Iranian operations remained purely defensive by nature – which puzzled the Iraqis. Before long, there was talk about replacing the two mechanized divisions of the II Corps with 11th Infantry Division.

The Crawl on Shush

Further south, 1st Mechanized Division – supported by 12 artillery batteries including one of BM-21 multiple rocket launchers (MRLs), took the border town of Fakkeh and – supported by 34th Armoured Brigade – then pushed across hilly terrain towards Shush. The Iraqis thus concentrated a force of more than 200 MBTs and 200 artillery pieces to attack an area protected by a mere 62 tanks and a dozen towed and self-propelled guns of the IRIA.[21] However, their advance was extremely slow; they first concentrated upon neutralising a handful of border posts before beginning to crawl eastwards, and eliminating IRIAF's forward ground installations – including several radar stations.

This slow advance created a threat to the northern flank of III Corps as it advanced through Susangerd, and prompted the 3rd Armoured Division to send its 12th Armoured Brigade northeast from Amarah for a 40-kilometre flanking movement – to threaten the defenders from the south. While capturing the IRIAF's crucial

The first phase of the Iran-Iraq War was one of great crisis for the Iranians. They had too few troops to occupy more than the most sensitive points along the front-lines, and had suffered heavy casualties. These Iranian infantrymen were photographed while evacuating an injured comrade. (Albert Grandolini Collection)

The Shi'a clergy did a lot to bolster the morale of the Iranian combatants right from the first days of the war. Here the future 'Supreme Leader of the Islamic Revolution', Ayatollah Sayyid Ali Hosseini Khamenei, with an officer of the Iranian Army during one of his visits of the frontlines. (Mark Lepko Collection)

radar site, on 2 October, the push was blocked near Chenaneh not only by the 37th Combat Group, but also two infantry battalions of 21st Division and the reconnaissance regiment of 92nd Armoured Division. The last significant Iraqi operation in this area in 1980 saw the 3rd Armoured Division inflict heavy losses upon the 2nd Brigade of the 92nd Armoured Division, leaving the Iranians demoralized. In turn, this enabled the Iraqis to establish good defensive positions along the upper Khark River, opposite Shush. However, they failed to secure the sand dune belt to the south which runs northeast of Bostan – because the III Corps on their right was bogged down in fighting around Susangerd.[22]

Iraqi I Corps in the Winter of 1980-1981

Despite their initial success, the Northern and Central Fronts remained relatively tense during the winter of 1980-1981, because Iraqi positions were constantly harassed by Iranian artillery and infantry raids. By 14 January 1981, reports emerged about 18th Infantry Brigade of the 4th Mountain Division and the 50th Armoured Brigade of the 12th Armoured Division showing signs of 'stress'; the few infantry units available were insufficient to properly secure the foothills around Ilam and the local road network became too dangerous even for movement of armoured fighting vehicles. The Iranians repeatedly infiltrated teams of jeep-mounted TOWs behind Iraqi positions and knocked out at least 35 MBTs over the time. Local Iraqi units also suffered from a lack of 130mm ammunition: their M-46 guns had to be replaced by 122mm pieces transferred from mountain divisions until sufficient stocks could be built-up.

Lacking other solutions, Iraqi Army Chief-of-Staff , Lieutenant-General Abd el-Jabbar Shahshal, suggested attaching Kurdish guerrillas to armoured units. The Director of the General Military Intelligence Directorate (GMID), Brigadier-General Abdul Jawad Dhannoun, supported this idea through a proposal to establish the so-called 'al-Jaf Group' – made p of about 1,500 Kurdish fighters from the Halabja area. However, Saddam not only preferred a much larger operation, but also recognized the threat of the Iranians destroying invading forces piecemeal.[23]

Overall, reflecting the priority on COIN – by direct or indirect means – the I Corps launched only two minor offensives during the winter of 1980-1981. In mid-December 1980, it struck southwest from Penjwin, attempting to capture the communications hub of Marivan and pre-empt any conventional threat to Sulaymaniyah. Advancing through rain, low cloud and mist on 18 December, it pushed some 50 kilometres into the foothills of the Zagros Mountains, encountering only weak resistance from 3rd Brigade of 28th Infantry Division, taking some 775 square kilometers with little loss. The Iranians reacted with air strikes and claim to have established air superiority over the region, which they should have held until the end of the war. However, the IRIAA lost at least one AH-1J, together with its pilot, Major-General Sharif Ashraf.[24]

Later the same month, 4th Mountain Division advanced two kilometers across the border from Halabja to the road junction of Nowsud (Nowdesheh), in support of the KDPI. The Iranian garrison – consisting of IRIA troops with some Pasdaran – was quickly driven out and the KDPI-leader Abdu Rahman Ghassemlou established his headquarters there. The Iranians counterattacked in Operation Mohammad Rasoolallah, on 2 January 1981, advancing some 5-6 kilometres despite bitter cold, strong winds, and heavy snow – only to be pushed out by an Iraqi counterattack.[25]

Despite the difficult weather, I Corps of the Iraqi Army staged another offensive around Nowsud and Penjwin, aiming to pin down enemy forces and erode their strength. On 21 Janaury 1981, 38th Infantry Brigade of 7th Infantry Division launched one raid, followed by another – involving 39th Infantry Brigade – on 15 February. Following the thaw, Iranian attacks pushed back the Iraqis

and on 29-31 May 1981 they struck 4th Mountain Division in the Penjwin sector, but were held by 29th Infantry Brigade. A similar effort in the Nowsud sector had the same effect. The Iranians attempted again on 2 July 1981, but lost most of their gains to Iraqi counter-attacks. The campaigning season in that year ended on 10 November, when 4th Mountain Division staged a successful pre-emptive attack on Iranian concentrations in the Nowsud region, despite heavy snow and low temperatures.[26]

II Corps' Problems

Starting from the night of 4/5 January 1981, the Iranians launched a small, diversionary offensive near Mehran and regained a few hundred metres of high ground in the upper valley of the Galal Badra. Five days later, they opened a month-long offensive by the Pasdaran – apparently their first large-scale offensive – targeting positions of 2nd Infantry Brigde, 2nd Infantry Division of the Iraqi Army. This resulted in the Iranians gaining control of the 12-kilometre-long Meimak Heights near Saif Saad. The success emboldened the Pasdaran to use large-scale infantry assaults as their battle-winning tactics in the future. Combined with the Iranian Operation Hoveyzeh, the IRGC's attack caused serious concerns for Saddam, who was worried that the Iranians might penetrate all the way to Baghdad. Certainly enough, Iranian harassing and diversionary operations not only confused the Iraqi leadership but erdoded the morale of their troops. Correspondingly, Defence Minister Adnan Kharaillah paid a three-day visit to the front, between 5 and 7 February 1981, as a result of which the brigade commander Lieutenant-Colonel Muhammad Juwad Kadhum and one of his company commanders were executed; the division commander Brigadier-General Hazem al-Barhawi was replaced by Brigadier-General Jawad Asad Shitna, while the commander of II Corps, Lieutenant-General Taha ash-Shakarji was replaced by Lieutenant-General Abd al-Jabar Abd ar-Rahim al-Asadi.[27] Furthermore, Saddam visited this frontline on 6 March, accompanied by King Hussein of Jordan, who witnessed the entry of the Jordanian 'al-Yarmouk Force' into the line.[28]

The rest of 1981 saw the II Corps concentrating primarily on the Qasr-e Shirin sector, where the Iranians launched several attempts to regain the town. The first was a week-long attack in the Dana Khushk heights, launched on the night of 22 to 23 April by the 7th Ghadir Brigade IRGC, supported by a tank battalion of 81st Division IRIA. The sector, that included peaks dominating the approaches to Qasr-e Shirin, was held by Major-General Salem Hussein al-Ali's 8th Infantry Division, and Brigadier-General Nizar Abd al-Karim al-Khazraji's 7th Infantry division, which replaced the 4th Mountain division. The 8th Division's 3rd Infantry Brigade had just replaced 22nd Infantry Brigade and was still unfamiliar with the territory, while other defenders were over-stretched, tired, and lacking reserves. Unsurprisingly, they were pushed back and it took the II Corps' major effort to retake Dana Khushk. This counterattack began on the night of 27-28 April 1981. The two infantry divisions were reinforced by the Republican Guards Brigade, 32nd Special Forces Brigade and the 6th Armoured Division, and saw the 7th Division fighting its way into the Dana Khushk from the south, while three other divisions swept along the road from Qasr-e Shirin to Sar-e Pol-e Zahab to regain most of the lost terrain. Even then, the Iranians retained their grip on Gilan-e Gharb and took 500 prisoners.[29]

Another Iranian attack – launched on the night of 3-4 September 1981 – drove 8th Infantry Division from much of the Sisar Heights, while 7th Infantry Division lost much of the Dana Khushk and the Kojar Pass. Further north, 6th Armoured Division had to

Illustrating the kind of problems both sides faced during the fighting in the northern sector of the Iran-Iraq War, this photograph shows a column of IRGC troops navigating one of the endless mountain chains in January 1982. (Tom Cooper Collection)

bring forward two brigades to stabilize the situation but it was the deployment of 32nd Special Forces Brigde that re-established the Iraqis in the Sisar range. The 7th Infantry Division – reinforced by the Special Forces Battalion of the Republican Guards – sought to regain the lost ground in the Dana Khushk, but with only limited success. Eventually, Baghdad had to accept that its Qasr e-Shirin garrison was exposed, and from mid October 1981 it began withdrawing troops from this area to reinforce the Dezful sector. Furthermore, 6th Armoured Division positioned its 25th Mechanized Brigade forward, while the remainder of its units were re-deployed upto 16 kilometres further west. This was a rather humiliating development considering that they faced only one depleted IRIA armoured brigade and various minor Pasdaran units.[30]

Operation Matla al-Fajr
On the central front, the year 1981 ended with a major Iranian offensive, Operation Matla al-Fajir (Rising of Dawn), launched on 11 December. Advancing through heavy rain, 81st Armoured Divison, 58th Commando Brigade, and a reinforced 7th Ghadir Pasdaran Brigade (totalling 14 battalions), attacked 2nd Infantry Brigade of 12th Armoured Division in the Summar sector. The following morning, the Iranians also assaulted the front and the right flank of 7th Infantry Division at Gilan-e Gharb and Qasr-e Shiring sector. As the battle descended into hand-to-hand fighting, the Iranians not only drove back the Iraqis, but also thwarted all counter-attacks. Only the second Iraqi effort – a counter-attack by 12th Armoured Division (now commanded by Brigadier-General Talal Khalil ad-Duri) – on the evening of 17 December 1981, regained most of the lost ground. Nevertheless, fighting continued and it was only on 5 January 1982 that the Iraqis re-took the last of their lost positions. Even then, the Iranians caught their breath and struck again, this time to the south, starting on 5 January, retaking Gilan-e Gharb. However, their thrust against Naft Shah was repulsed.[31]

In an attempt to bolster the morale, Saddam then gave a speech claiming his army could take any place. In order to demonstrate this, 10th Armoured Division was ordered to take Dehloran. This created a task force centred around 17th Armoured Brigade, and attacked during the night of 28-29 May. The Iraiqs took the town, but lacked infantry to hold it and were forced to withdraw only 12 hours later.[32]

Further south, the III Corps spent most of the winter of 1980-1981 strengthening defensive positions, improving the roads, and constructing supply dumps. Sorkheh was developed into a major stronghold, but then the Iraqis recognized that two mechanized divisions were unsuitable for holding the area and forward-deployed reserve brigades in their place.

The Iranian side of the frontline was held by 1st Brigade of 21st Infantry Divison (Dezful sector) and 2nd Brigade of 92nd Armoured Division (Shush sector). These totaled only some 100 MBTs and some 70 artillery pieces, and thus did very little. Between 3 and 21 April 1981, 21st Infantry Division attacked the two Iraqi reserve brigades and took their positions, but then the front went largely quiet for the rest of the year.[33]

CHAPTER 2
PRIVATE WARS

Although part of a greater struggle, many operations by both sides on the northern and central fronts had the characteristics of private wars. These were fought in a wide range of terrain and, unlike the big battles on the southern front, were characterized by the absence of a continuous line.

In areas where they were constructed, frontlines wound high into the mountains, until reaching elevations and areas where they rather resembled scattered battalion- and then company-strongpoints. Most positions in the mountains were based on stone breastworks (sangars); except in the summer, these were bitterly cold, and vulnerable to heavy snow falls or torrential rains that occasionally triggered avalanches or land slips. The latter two also kept both sides constantly busy with repairing their roads.

Fighting in such terrain required top physical fitness – not only because of the rugged terrain but also due to the rare air and frequent supply problems. Four-wheel-drive vehicles could move supplies over many of the minor roads and even hillside tracks but, with few helicopters for resupply, mule trains remained the prime means of moving food and ammunition. The mountainous terrain also presented radio communication problems: the use of FM radios was restricted by limited horizontal and vertical line-of-sight, while UHF radio signals could be 'bent' to leap over mountain tops – all provided the transceivers were positioned high enough. Multiple peaks would usually thwart their transmissions.

Iranian Army Organization

On the Iranian side the defence was originally based upon scattered, understrength, IRIA formations augmented by Gendarmerie and Police. New command arrangements were created under the Supreme Defence Council (SDC), with representatives of the government and the armed forces, and between 1984 and 1986 when several brigades were expanded into divisions. The IRIA Ground Forces command then created two Forward Operational Headquarters (FOHQ); the Northern (NFOHQ) with headquarters in Torbat-e Heydariyeh, northwest of Urmia, with a forward HQ near Sumar; and the Central (CFOHQ) at Kermanshah. The right wing of the Southern Front (SFOHQ) was semi-autonomous.[34]

The NFOHQ controlled the 28th, 30th and 64th Infantry Division IRIA, the 11th Artillery Group, and – later on – the 23rd Special Forces Division, with a total of some 80,000 troops by 1988. The CFOHQ eventually received the 58th and 84th Infantry; the 81st and 88th Armoured Divisions; 37th Armoured, 40th Infantry, and 55th Airborne Brigades; and 191st Combat Group and 44th Artillery Group – with a total of about 91,000 troops. The Dezful sector controlled the 16th Armoured, 21st and 77th Infantry Divisions, and 22nd Artillery Group with a total of no less than 61,000 troops, but would often detach brigades to the southern Front.[35] The IRIAA usually operated detachments from the 1st, 2nd, and 3rd Combat Support Groups (CSGs) and the 4th and 5th General Support Groups (GSGs) close to the frontline. All major army formations were usually reinforced with ad hoc Qods battalions before they began benefitting from the expansion of the IRGC.

The Dezful sector was often 'milked' to aid its neighbours: at least one brigade of 16th Armoured Division and one or two brigades of 21st and 77th Divisions were usually attached to the SFOHQ, while in 1984 they were temporarily joined by most of the NFOHQ's 28th Division and a brigade of the 81st Division. The security situation in the north necessitated the return of the 28th Division in November 1984, but the poor transport network meant such movements took an inordinate amount of time. For example, moving 81st Division to new positions in CFOHQ took almost two months. Therefore, most of the IRIA divisions acted as static sector commands.

Gendarmerie and Pasdaran

Supporting the IRIA was the Iranian Islamic Gendarmerie under the Interior Ministry and responsible for law enforcement in rural areas and border patrols. It strength had dropped from 75,000 before the Revolution to 40,000 (mostly due to conscripts leaving) and it was organised into some 250 companies assigned to 16 districts – each with two to five 'regiments.' The Gendarmerie was primarily armed with small arms, mortars, and light anti-armour weapons, but had a few BTR-60 wheeled APCs, and excellent communication systems. Therefore, it was often deployed to support combat operations in the north.

Iranian troops, with a Chieftain MBT, somewhere in the Dezful sector in 1981. (via N. S.)

An Iranian soldier guarding four Scorpion light tanks, somewhere on the central front, during the first winter of the Iran-Iraq War. A squadron of Scorpions was assigned to the reconnaissance regiment of each Iranian Army division. (via N. S.)

The Gendarmerie also shielded the road network near the border from guerrillas and Special Forces, but proved not particularly successful due to the terrain. The IRIA berated the Gendarmerie para-military force for its failures, and a number of minor operations to take heights to the west were motivated by necessity to keep related problems in check, as much as with the crushing of the Kurdish revolt (which ended only in 1983).

As in the south, the Revolutionary Guards began deploying ever larger light infantry formations within the NFOHQ and CFOHQ, starting in 1982, but they never deployed as many of their troops in these areas as they did in the south. Through mid-1980s, the Pasdaran created specialised support formations – such as artillery and engineers – from infantry units. It was during this period that the 45th Javad ol-Aemeh and 46th al-Haadi Engineer Divisions, and the 89th Moharram Artillery Brigade came into being. There followed specialized infantry formations like the 6th Imam Sadeq Commando Division, the 77th Nabbovat Commando and 622nd Beit-ol-Moghadddas Mountain Brigades. Even then, the number of such formations remained very limited; as of 1988 US intelligence assessed the total IRGC manpower with the NFOHQ at only 20,000, and that with the CFOHQ at 30,000. By contrast, the Pasdaran formations in Dezful sector alone totalled about 68,000. It was only following the disastrous attempts to take Basra – Operations Val Fajr-4/5/8 – that Tehran decided to switch attention to the Northern Front and transferred about a dozen of divisions and brigades (total of about 100,000 troops) from the SFOHQ to the NFOHQ.[36]

Raids and Reconnaissance Operations

The rugged terrain in the north provided opportunities for deep reconnaissance, raiding and sabotage operations. At first the Iranians used special forces teams from 23rd Commando Brigade, sometimes reinforced by teams from 55th Airborne Brigade. However, the IRIA's participation in Special Operations was gradually restricted. Instead, it was its SIGINT base at Sanandaj – which had staff fluent in English, different Kurdish dialects, Arabic and Russian – which became ever more important.[37]

It was the Pasdaran which assumed the lead in Special Operations. In the mid-1980s, they established their 66th Vali-ye-Amr and 75th Zhafar Special Forces Brigades (both were part of Pasdaran military intelligence). Furthermore, as Tehran's relations with the Iraqi Kurds improved, in 1986 the Ramadan Guerrilla Warfare Headquarters (RGWHQ) was established. Supported by the IRIAA, this command of the IRGC included its two special forces brigades and the 67th Brigade, trained specifically to attack oil pipelines. However, this unit launched only a few operations before Turkish diplomatic pressure forced Tehran to stop targeting such installations; indeed, it might have resulted in disbandment of the latter unit.

Nevertheless, the RGWHQ organized cross-border supplies for the Iraqi Kurds and began co-ordinating their operations to a degree where nearly all major Kurdish operations of the late 1980s appear to have been devised in, and directed from, Iran. Furthermore, this headquarters supported such non-Kurdish groups as insurgents of the Dawa Party, and had one of their units attached to the 9th Badr Division IRGC.

Iraqi Reorganisations

On the Iraqi side I and II Corps were initially responsible for command and control on the two fronts. However, as the Iranians recovered and began exercising pressure upon the whole frontline, the Iraqis found themselves forced to reorganize. After realising that the II Corps held a frontline of no less than 460 kilometres, Saddam ordered the establishment of IV Corps under Major-General Hisham Sabah al-Fakhri, with its HQ in al-Amarah. This took over the 1st Mechanized and 10th Armoured Division from the III Corps, and became responsible for operations in Wasit and Maysan Provinces. The II Corps' front was reduced to southern Diyala, while the I Corps' frontline was limited to operations in Arbil, Sulaymaniyah, and northern Diyala.[38]

The lack of a separate command for the relatively quiet Wasit province remained a problem. In 1984 the responsibility for this area was transferred to the 'East of Tigris Operations Headquarters' (ETOH), but the growing threat in the Hawaizeh Marshes saw it returned to the south. Finally, in September 1986 a unique solution was found in establishing the I Special Corps, headquartered in al-Kut under Lieutenant-General Ismael Tayeh an-Nuaimi. Nauaimi controlled three volunteer divisions and a special commando brigade consisting of retired officers and reservists, most of them older than 39.[39]

While such reorganizations helped improve the control of conventional operations, the northern front in particular continued facing a growing unconventional threat, especially in the form of Iranian-supported Kurdish insurgency. The need both to run a counter-insurgency campaign and interdict Kurdish supply lines across northern Iraq led to the creation of Northern Operations Headquarters (Quaidet Amaliyat ash-Shamaliyah, NOHQ) under Major-General Dhiya ad-Din Jala, in the summer of 1985. This was responsible for operations along the Turkish border in Arbil,

Many commando operations on the northern sector of the frontlines involved heliborne insertion of the involved troops. Here an IRGC-unit is waiting its turn to embark upon a CH-47C Chinook helicopter of the IRIAA. (IRIAA)

This photograph shows a Bell 214A helicopter of the IRIAA deploying troops on another 'strategically important' peak. (IRIAA)

Dahuk and Ninaws provinces, and was later upgraded to the status of V Corps (HQ in Arbil). Unlike the Southern Front, local commanders were frequently rotated. This was Saddam's decision, aimed at preventing officers from creating power bases. However, others were removed for failures – including brave, staunch and proven members of the Ba'ath Party – like Major-Generals Taha Nuri Yasi ash-Shakarji and Sultan Hashim Ahmed al-Jaburi at-Tai. Furthermore, Major-General Abd al-Aziz Ibrahim al-Hadithi was killed on 22 January 1988, when his helicopter crashed in bad weather.

The greatest changes took place in 1987-1988, when former commander of I Corps, Nizar Abd al-Karim al-Khazraji became Chief-of-Staff and began to re-organise the Iraqi Army in preparation for driving the Iranians back across the border. Although a Ba'athist, Khazraji was an extremely able commander and a key feature of his new strategy was to create a massive GHQ reserve by stripping most of the corps' reserves – a concept which Saddam accepted but which had to be 'sold' to the corps commanders. Most accepted this but II Corps' Lieutenant General Shawkat Ahmed Ata and I Special Corps neighbour Lieutenant General Ismail Taya al-Nuaimi remained strongly opposed. Saddam's reaction was to replace Ata (a competent but overcautious officer who lost the Faw Peninsula in 1987) with Kamel Sajet Aziz al-Janabi and Nuaimi (one of Iraq's longest-serving officers), and then another retiree – Lieutenant General Kamal Jamil Aboud. Another, more delicate, command problem occurred before the 'Tawakkalna ala Allah 3' in the summer of 1988. The IV Corps commander Lieutenant General Muhammad Abd al-Qadir Abd al-

The Year 1982 was one of major Iranian victories on several battlefields of the Iran-Iraq War. This Iraqi OT-62 (Czechoslovak-made BTR-50 APC) slipped off bridge during often panicky retreat. (via N. S.)

A group of captured Iraqi troops as seen at one of collection points behind Iranian lines in 1982. (via N. S.)

Rahman had been responsible for much of the earlier planning for this operation, but Director of Operations, General Hussein Rashid Al Tikriti and the Director of Military Intelligence General Sabir al Duri – who may have feared that another success by Qadir would make him the next candidate for the post of the Army's Chief-of-Staff (which they also coveted) – wanted him transferred to VII Corps, and replaced by the equally competent Lieutenant General Ayad Khlil Zaki. Defence Minister General Adnan Khairallah Telfah (Kairallah) wanted Qadir to remain in place at least until the new offensive finished. Eventually a compromise was reached; Qadir remained at IV Corps acting as standby for Ayad Khlil Zaki.[40]

Expansion of the Iraqi Army

Iraq's original dozen divisions were inadequate for a prolonged war, and new ones were created – most of these infantry formations. Furthermore, the crisis of the southern front in summer of 1982 saw three divisions from I and II Corps (4th Mountain, 6th Armoured,

and 11th Infantry) sent south. As compensation the 17th Armoured Division was formed in II Corps.

Between 1982 and 1986, 26 division-sized formations were created in the Northern and Central Fronts. Many were raised by expanding ad hoc formations like Ash-Shib Force (18th Div), Arbil Defence Force (23rd Div), Kirkuk Defence Force (24th Div), Jilat Force (25th Div), Darband-i-Khan Force (36th Div) and Shahibi Force (37th Div). Others – including the 43rd, 44th and 45th – were divisional task forces (Kiadat Kuwat) sometimes controlling brigades on an ad hoc basis, but with smaller support elements. Nominally, each new division had three brigades and often a commando battalion; in reality, the divisions acted as task force headquarters which could control up to 10 or more brigades with up to 26,000 troops. During a review of Northern Front operations on 26 May 1988, Khazraji noted that of 132 infantry brigades (including 16 special forces/commando formations) about half were within the NFOHQ, of which I Corps had 42, while V Corps had 15.[41]

Each corps had its own troops, including an artillery brigade, an air defence brigade, reconnaissance, engineer and bridging battalions. Corps commands also created up to two commando brigades as their intervention forces, and often augmented these with some of GHQ's special forces formations – created from the three original units. Commando brigades of I and V Corps were used for COIN operations too. Ground troops were supported by the Iraqi Army Aviation Corps (IrAAC), which provided units equipped with gunships and transport helicopters, but also squadrons equipped with Pilatus PC-7 light attack aircraft. Nominally, 1st Wing was headquartered in Kirkuk (it supported I and V Corps); 2nd Wing in Baghdad (it supported II and I Special Corps); and 4th Wing at Amara (it supported IV and VI Corps).[42]

Khazraji's demand for strengthening GHQ reserves was reinforced when the Iranians launched their Val Fajr-10 offensive around Lake Darband-i-Khan in March 1988. The destruction of 43rd Division created the need to reinforce I Corps and 28th Infantry Division, 70th and 80th Armoured Brigade (17th Armoured Division), and 46th Mechanized Brigade (12th Armoured Division) were all rushed up from II Corps, together with corps troops from IV Corps.[43] Their arrival helped to stabilise the front while the Iraqi Army was running a number of major offensives on the southern front in summer 1988.

For covert operations Baghdad relied upon its special forces, but also had two units of the GMID, created with Egyptian assistance in 1984, Units 888 and 999, each of some 800 officers and other ranks. The former unit was responsible for gathering intelligence and running sabotage operations with the help of sympathetic Iranians and Iranian Kurds; the latter unit was a deep reconnaissance formation similar to the British Special Air Service.[44] Finally, the GMID developed an extensive SIGINT infrastructure – although this proved less effective in tracking IRGC's units – primarily because of Iranian chronical shortage of radios.

Iraqi Para-Military Organizations

The Iraqi Army was supported by two para-military organisations. The 48,000-strong Border Guard (operated by the Ministry of Defence since February 1980, before reverting to the Ministry of Interior in March 1985), was organized into 24 brigades with three battalions of light infantry each. The Border Guard often supported the military in conventional and COIN operations, and – in low-level urban security duties – was augmented by the police and the Popular Army of the Ba'ath Party (al-Jaysh ash-Shabi).[45]

Rural areas of northern Iraq were the responsibility of the Kurdish militia – or Command of the National Defense Battalions (NDBs), nicknamed the Fursan Salahuldin (Saladin's Knights) – but also known as 'Young Donkeys' between Kurdish insurgents. Originally raised in the 1960s, the NDBs were primarily for internal security duties but also they were to attract men who might otherwise join the insurgents.[46] The NDBs were usually raised voluntarily – sometimes under pressure – by tribal leaders anxious to demonstrate their loyalty to Baghdad, or to strengthen their local standing. By 1987, there were 147 NDBs with – nominally – some 205,000 troops, or some 10% of the Kurdish population. Their number continued increasing and by August 1988 no less than 321 battalions should have been operational, totalling 412,636 troops. Correspondingly, starting in 1986, some NDBs were grouped into divisional-sized commands known as National Defence Headquarters, of which six were created within the areas of responsibility of I and V Corps by the end of the war.[47]

Each NDB was under the command of an advisor/consultant

T-55 MBTs of the Iraqi Army, in a typical position surrounded by earthen berms, somewhere along the central frontline in 1984 or 1985. (Tom Cooper Collection)

Youthful troops of one of the many of ad hoc units of the Iraqi Army converted into regular divisions in mid-1980s. Many of the resulting divisions were armed with older weapons, and lacked their full complement of artillery and other support elements. (Albert Grandolini Collection)

(Mustashar), selected by the clan or tribal leader, who – like all the troops – received a salary and was also paid for each man on his roster (which encouraged inflated strength returns). Indeed, one battalion was disbanded by the General Security Department (GSD) when it was discovered to have only 90 men and not the 500 claimed.

Many Kurds joined the NDBs to avoid being drafted into the Iraqi Army, but they had no enthusiasm for Baghdad and suffered a high desertion and absenteeism rate; 82,957 in the NFOHQ between August 1985 and March 1987. Unsurprisingly, five of battalions were disbanded for related reasons in 1987 alone. The GSD closely monitored the NDBs for signs of rebellion or defection, with suspected Mustashars sometimes being executed – one after he planned to assassinate the V Corps commander! To reduce the risk of defection or desertion, NBDs were frequently rotated between different areas, but this didn't help; defections continued and thus drastic consequences were introduced for families of deserters – including deportation and/or imprisonment. On the other hand, those that did join the NDB were considered pariahs among the Kurds. Correspondingly, their reliability was always of concern to the Ba'ath Party, which in October 1986 bitterly complained about their commitment, willingness to surrender, provide intelligence to the enemy, and to destroy or sell military equipment.[48]

The Ba'ath Party exercised the control over two 'elite' Kurdish COIN units – each of about 1,000 troops. One was the Emergency Force and responsible for urban COIN, while the other was the Special Unit, operated by the General Security Directorate (Amn),

A group of combatants of the MEK/MKO seen during their training. This organisation was widely publicised by the Iraqis, in attempt to discredit the government in Tehran through presenting 'Iranians fighting on the side of Iraq'. (Albert Grandolini Collection)

The MEK/MKO included plenty of females and was keen to present these in the public. The group was foremost a political force, and was rarely deployed in combat before 1988. (Albert Grandolini Collection)

and responsible for rural counter-intelligence. To counter-balance these two, the Ba'ath created the Light Battalions in 1984, but these, 'soon became a haven for deserters and volunteers looking to make a living and obtain arms'.[49]

Iranian Exiles

The two Iraqi fronts facing Iranians in the north and centre received the mixed blessings of the presence of the National Liberation Army (Artesh-e Azadibakhsh Melli Iran) – the military arm of the Mujahidden e-Khalq (MeK) Iranian resistance movement. The NLA was founded on 20 June 1987, led by Massoud Rajavi but actually commanded by Mahmoud Ataii, this organization was

considered 'terrorist' in Iran, but rapidly grew in size. By 1988, it included 10 full divisions with 35 combat and support brigades (two entirely staffed by female personnel). Nominally totalling about 180,000 troops supported by armour, artillery, and engineering units, the NLA was actually about 20,000 strong, and little more than a politically-led militia raised from defectors, emigres and a few prisoners of war, lacking professional leadership and training. Over time, and due to participation in some conventional operations, some of its units matched those of the IRGC's Basiji and Pasdaran. However, most of the NLA spent the war inside camps around Baghdad, passing time by posing in highly-publicised parades – described as 'inefficient' and 'scruffy' by most of foreign observers.[50]

CHAPTER 3
THE CENTRAL FRONT 1982-1987

By the New Year of 1982 the newly-established IV Corps held a salient west of Dezful and Shush some 75 kilometres long and 40 kilometres deep, which then merged near Bostan into a narrow (20 kilometre) wide strip of Iranian territory leading into the Hawizah Marshes. Sandy desert seemed to secure the northern and southern flanks although the Iranian Operation Tarigh al-Qods had demonstrated this was not impassable, especially not for the Pasdaran. Meanwhile, II Corps still under Aziz at Ba'qubah was left with (north-to-south) 8th Infantry, 7th and 2nd Mountain Divisions with 12th Armoured Division. It was in this area that the Iranians launched their first major offensives on the central front, resulting in several disasters for the Iraqis.

Early in 1982, Tehran decided to cut off out what it perceived as the 'Iraqi cancers in its holy territory' with two major consecutive offensives: Operation Fatah al-Mobin (Clear or Undeniable Victory) – usually called Operation 'Fatah' – and Operation Beit-ol-Mogaddas. The former was to hit IV Corps' salient opposite Dezful and Shush, while the latter was to hit III Corps.

The battlefield stretched between the River Doveyrich (Duveryrij/Dwayrij/Doiraj), some 8-16 kilometres to the east, and the River Kharakeh (Karkha or Kharkha), some 50 kilometres deeper inside Iran. On its norther side were the foothills of the Kabirkuh, some 200-500 metres high and occupied by the Iranians, while in the south was a belt of sand dunes around the Mishdagh Hills. The terrain in between was largely open, undulating ground, but behind

the northern face of the Iraqi salient was the Movazi Ridge.

Operation 'Fatah al-Mobin'

Iranian planning was in the capable hands of the IRIA's Chief of Staff, General Sayed Shirazi, a shrewd tactician who was nominated Commander of the Ground Forces, and was aided by the fact that the Iranian positions overlooked the enemy defences. Due to the southern front being a tougher nut to crack, Tehran decided to launch Fatah, a double envelopment of IV Corps, first. Once this had sucked in enemy reserves the Iranians would strike into the underbelly from the south to isolate, then annihilate, the enemy. Preparations began in December 1981 and to secure Pasdaran support, Shirazi successfully enlisted the help of President Ali Hosseini Khamenei, which meant the main theme of a Pasdaran commander seminar held in Tehran during January 1982 was co-operation with the IRIA together with organising and controlling mass attacks.

Four Task Forces were created (see Table 2 for details) with Qods and Nasr in the north, and Fajr and Fath in the east. The northern assault consisted of six IRIA brigades and four Pasdaran divisions, and was supported by an independent tank company and 44th Artillery Group (total of 17 batteries with 100 artillery pieces).[51] The eastern assault was to involve six IRIA brigades and seven Pasdaran divisions, and was supported by 33rd Artillery Group (12 batteries with 70 guns). All the troops involved in the assault used

Sayed Ali Shirazi, Chief of Staff of the Iranian Army. (Tom Cooper Collection)

Large-scale operations of the Iranian ground forces on the central and northern fronts of the war with Iraq were usually supported by one or more of the IRIAA's Combat Support Groups, each of which included a company of Boeing CH-47C Chinook heavy helicopters. (IRIAA)

full-scale mock-ups of Iraqi strongpoints to practice attacks. The assault force totalled some 47,000 Army, 65,000 Pasdaran and 10,000 Basiji troops, supported by 270 MBTs, 170 artillery pieces, 64 attack and assault helicopters, and 12 Boeing CH-47C Chinook medium transport helicopters.[52]

Iraqi Preparations

Iraqi intelligence quickly detected signs of Iranian preparations and the assembly of a dozen IRIA brigades. However, the shadowy presence of the Pasdaran was at least as much a reason for uncertainty as for anything else. COMINT played a major role in Iraqi intelligence, and this proved capable of decrypting some of the IRIA's code. However, the Pasdaran lacked radios and relied upon land-line communications or couriers, which the Iraqis were unable to monitor. The GMID should have been able to gauge precise Iranian intentions through the assembly of bridging equipment, but it remained uncertain as to whether this was a diversion or a major thrust. To make sure, in early March 1982, Baghdad provided Fakhri with substantial reinforcements – including 3rd Armoured Division (Brigadier-General Juwad Assad Shetna) and 10th Armoured Brigade, together with several artillery batteries from GHQ's and III Corps reserves, while II Corps sent its 9th Armoured Division south, too.

Fakhri already had 1st Mechanized, 10th Armoured (Brigadier-General Thabit Sultan), 11th and 14th Infantry Divisions holding the northern shoulder of the salient, and 1st Mechanized Division (Brigadier-General Thamir Hamad Mahmoud) the southern shoulder. Part of the 11th Infantry Division held the sector covering Bostan, while the 14th Infantry held the line into the Hawizeh Marshes. However, neither they nor Fakhri's reaction force – 32nd

Special Forces Brigade – would be involved in the disaster. Overall, the salient's defences ran along the River Kharkhekh, from Dasht-e Abbs in the north to Mishdagh Hills in the south, and were manned by 86,000 troops supported by 1,500 MBTs, and 400 artillery pieces.

The III Corps' experiences had demonstrated the inadequacy of mechanised formations in static defence (see Volume 1), so the mechanised divisions were given eight infantry brigades – many of them staffed by reservists recently recalled to the colours. Sultan deployed not only five infantry brigades but also his two armoured brigades in static positions on his left, leaving only the 24th Mechanized Brigade in reserve. Hamad had three infantry brigades and one mechanized brigade in line behind one of largest minefields ever constructed by the Iraqis, while his reserve – 1st Mechanized and 34th Armoured Brigades – was east of Fakkeh. All of their defensive positions consisted of the usual triangular battalion-strongpoints, which in the east and south were buttressed with berms. Because the Iraqi Army was overstretched, many of the key communication hubs behind the lines were held by Popular Army troops, a somewhat slender reed, a large number of which were reportedly incorporated in 1st Mechanized Division's defences.[53]

Table 2: Order of Battle for Operation Fath al-Mobin, March 1982

Corps	Division	Brigades
Iran		
Task Force Qods	84th Infantry Division IRIA	3 brigades
	92nd Armoured Division IRIA	2nd Brigade
	14th Imam Hossein Infantry Division IRGC	3 brigades
	41st Sarallah Infantry Division IRGC	
Task Force Nasr	21st Infantry Division IRIA	1st, 2nd, 3rd Brigades (10 battalions)
	58th Infantry Brigade IRIA	
	7th Vali-e-Asr Infantry Division IRGC	3 brigades
	27th Mohammad Rasoolallah Infantry Brigade IRGC	

Task Force Fajr	77th Infantry Division IRIA	1st, 2nd and 3rd Brigades
	17th Ali Ibn Abu Talib Infantry Division IRGC	
	33rd Ali Mahdi Infantry Division IRGC	
	35th Imam Hassan Infantry Division IRGC	
	46th al-Haadi Infantry Brigade IRGC	
Task Force Fatah	92nd Armoured Division IRIA	1st Brigade
	37th Armoured Brigade IRIA	
	55th Airborne Brigade IRIA	
	3rd Saheb az-Zaman Infantry Division IRGC	
	8th Najaf Ashraf Infantry Division IRGC	
	25th Karbala Infantry Division IRGC	
Other units	33rd & 44th Artillery Group IRIA	
	2nd & 3rd CSGs, IRIAA	
Iraq		
IV Corps	Corps troops, including IV Corps Artillery Brigade	
	1st Mechanised Division	34th & 51st Armoured Brigades; 1st & 27th Mechanised Brigades; 93rd, 96th, 109th & 426th Infantry Brigades
	10th Armoured Division	17th & 42nd Armoured Brigades; 24th Mechanised Brigade; 55th, 99th, 423rd & 505th Infantry Brigades
Reserves	3rd Armoured Division	6th & 12th Armoured Brigades; 8th Mechanised Brigade
	9th Armoured Division	35th & 43rd Armoured Brigades, 14th Mechanised Brigades
	10th Armoured Brigade	
	5th Border Guards Brigade	
	2nd Wing IrAAC	

The Onslaught

Anticipating an attack on the Iranian New Year (Norouz), 21 March 1982, the two Iraqi divisions launched a pre-emptive attack, Operation al-Fowz al-Azim (Glorious Victory). In the course of this enterprise, run from 19 to 21 March, each division deployed one brigade-sized task force. The 1st Mechanized Division's 34th Armoured Brigade drove 15 kilometres deep before withdrawing, and both sides lost heavily but the Iraqis calculated that their efforts had been successful. They did not anticipate a new assault, but the Iranian time-table was not significantly affected.[54]

Iraqi complacency was dashed at 0330hrs on 22 March 1982 – exactly 18 months after their invasion and the day after Norouz – when the Iranians launched Fatah with a stunning blow from the north. Operating as battlegroups some 15 kilometres apart, Iranian task forces – spearheaded by Pasdaran light infantry – exploited the hilly terrain to infiltrate Iraqi positions, then used the hills to shield them from armoured counterattacks, while enjoying fire-support of the IRIA. Careful reconnaissance enabled the Iranians to target positions manned by reservist units, and religious fervour carried the advancing infantry – which advanced in 1,000-strong, brigade-waves at half-mile intervals, urged on by mullahs who showed no regard for their own safety – ever further forward. An Iraqi officer later said;

> They came at us like a crowd coming out of a mosque on a Friday. Soon we were firing into dead men, some draped over the barbed wire fences, and others in piles on the ground, having stepped on mines.[55]

Actually, the Iranian attack was much more sophisticated, and included a heliborne landing of Iranian Special Forces behind positions of 10th Armoured Division. These overran Iraqi batteries on Hill 651 which had been shelling the TFB.4 and Dezful, and destroyed or captured up to 30 130mm M-46 guns. Simultaneously, IRIA's 21st Infantry Division and 84th Infantry Brigade punched holes in the Iraqi line and isolated both of Sultan's armoured brigades before capturing the road junction of Chananeh, just 200 metres of 3rd Armoured Division's command post. The Iranian armour, fighter-bombers and helicopter gunships hit hard with everything available. The IRIAF flew at least 95 combat sorties, to which the IRIAA added over 100; their crews, and the army's tanks claimed between 320 and 400 Iraqi tanks knocked out during the morning. The luckless defenders were thus assaulted from all directions and pinned down; subsequent estimates concluded that 90% of the Iranian attacks overran their objectives.[56] Facing Iranian summons to surrender, the commander of 42nd Armoured Brigade, Colonel Iyad Futaykh Khalifa ar-Rawi, reacted by issuing each of his officers two hand grenades – one for the enemy and one for themselves. His unit took three days of bitter fight to break out, followed by 17th Armoured Brigade.

The collapse of the Iraqi northern line exposed both of Thamir Hamad's mechanized brigades which were both mauled in 'clumsy and confused' attempts at mobile defence. Despite Saddam's demands that units stand or fall in their positions, the northern defenders began to abandon the hills, and retreated some 10 kilometres compounding Fakhri's woes. Their withdrawal allowed the Iranians to bring their guns onto the heights and strike the Iraqi rear. The IrAF and IrAAC attempted to intervene, and their pilots claimed as many as 196 Iranian MBTs but most of their sorties were ineffective due to general confusion on the ground.

Iraqi Collapse

Despite the air support, Fakhri recognised he was in a desperate situation and ordered both divisions to make an orderly withdrawal, starting with 10th Armoured Division. However, Thamir Hamad then wrecked the plan. He had always been a weak commander

Once mobilized and deployed on the frontlines, the Iranian Army became capable of putting sizeable formations of its armour on the battlefield – including weak brigades equipped with British-made Chieftain MBTs, two of which are visible on this pre-war photograph. (Albert Grandolini)

While relatively small in total numbers of available tubes, and often suffering from lack of ammunition early during the war, the Iranian artillery played a crucial role in supporting offensive operations. This photograph is showing a pair of M109A1s early in the morning before a major fire operation. (Albert Grandolini Collection)

and exacerbated the crisis by moving his headquarters to the rear. Just as the northern forces began to withdraw, he ordered his two remaining brigades to do the same. As soon as he learned the news Fakhri ordered the brigades to remain in place, but the confused troops panicked. Hamad then lost all semblance of control of his men and they abandoned positions held since October 1980, fleeing to Fakkeh which became a scene of utter chaos. The situation was brought under control only once the Iraqi officers finally realized that the Iranians had halted – probably because their own supply system had collapsed.

With 3rd Armoured Division headquarters under attack, Fakhri had to cover the withdrawal by personally directing counter-attacks. Initially, he used 10th Armoured Brigade's T-72s and 24th Mechanized Brigade to support the 17th and 60th Armoured Brigades, artillery barrages and MRLs to stop the Iranian advance on Eyn Kush on 22 March 1982. However, the increasingly desperate situation in the south led to most of his units being re-deployed there, and being replaced only by the Mechanized Brigade of the Republican Guards. Counter-attacks by this formation, and other

reserves, usually dissolved into frontal assaults on strongest Iranian positions and were stopped with ease.[57]

Heavy losses forced Fakhri to rob Peter to pay Paul; he stripped 1st Mechanized Division of troops used to prop up the frontlines, in turn weakening positions of this unit. Renewed Iranian attacks on 23 March 1982 then forced him to deploy elements of 3rd Armoured Division to shore up the 1st Mechanized, and re-route the 10th and 12th Armoured Brigades to face a new threat coming from the Mishdagh Hills. The two units counter-attacked on 24 March, with heavy artillery support and several FROG-7 rockets, but the Iranians counterattacked and isolated the 12th, forcing it to fight out of the encirclement. The only positive action of the Iraqis on this day was the IrAF's effort to stop the advance of 25th Karbala Division IRGC on Chenaneh; this was hit by up to 150 strikes, and forced to entrench.

Crisis for Saddam

On 24 March 1982, Saddam Hussein arrived on the front leading a high-ranking delegation (including the Defence Minister and

An Iranian Army Chieftain MBT passing by a column of captured Iraqi troops during Operation Fatah al-Mobbin. (Tom Cooper Collection)

The Iranian counter-offensives in 1982 were better supported than ever before. Between others, the IRIAF deployed its British-made Rapier SAMs to improve the protection of ground forces. This firing unit was photographed somewhere in the Urumiyeh area, in March 1982. (IRIAF)

Chief of Staff). He dismissed Thamir Hamid and then personally supervised the restoration of the situation for three days. Amongst others, he ordered a re-deployment of a brigade from 12th Armoured Division in Khorramshar, and another from 7th Infantry Division at Qasr-e Shirin. Such measures proved ineffective and Saddam was nearly captured when his convoy was ambushed while inspecting the frontline.[58]

The situation further deteriorated during the night of 24-25 March, when the Iranians hit Fakhri's right flank with a powerful concentration of 88th and 92nd Armoured Division, 55th Airborne Brigade, and several of the IRGC's brigades.[59] A night later, the Iranians hit 1st Mechanized Division too, inflicting heavy casualties. However, their supply system collapsed again and thus they lost the momentum and were unable to exploit the chaos they caused. Nevertheless, by the morning of 27 March, the Iranians liberated Hill 651 and thus completed the elimination of the Iraqi threat to TFB.4. In a matter of few hours, the IRIAF then brought in a battery of MIM-23B I-HAWK and British-made Rapier SAMs; this soon inflicted losses to the IrAF.[60]

Eventually, Saddam was left without a choice but to authorise construction of new defences closer to the international border, along a 20-kilometre-long strip anchored on its southern side on the dune belt, before arcing north of Bostan and Fakkeh, and then following the River Doveyrich. The Iranians followed the Iraqi withdrawal for a few kilometres before starting to consolidate their gains on 29 March. Immediately afterwards, they began moving most of their forces further south – to the Ahwaz-Abadan theatre of operations.

The Iraqis exploited the resulting end of the battle by scrutinizing their officers. Reportedly, several of Thamir Hamid's subordinated were jailed or executed. By contrast, any criticism of Fakhri was muted; he retained his command until 1983 when he was appointed the Head of the Intelligence Agency (Mukhabarat) and replaced by Lieutenant-General Thabit Sultan Ahmed.

Aftermath

Operation Fatah al-Mobin was a tremendous victory – bigger than the Iranians had ever expected. It effectively swept IV Iraqi Corps out of Iran, mauled two armoured and one mechanized divisions – a total of 12 brigades – and captured up to 15,450 prisoners, 320-350 MBTs, about 100 other Armoured Fighting Vehicles (AFVs), 165-200 guns, and an entire battery of SA-6 SAMs. The booty allowed the Pasdaran to create their first 10 artillery batteries and their first armoured brigade on 1 April 1982. An emboldened deputy commander of 21st Division IRIA exclaimed, 'Now we are going to write our own manuals, with absolutely new tactics that the Americans and British and French can study at their staff colleges'. Although Joint Chief of Staff, General Zahir-Nejad, officially disavowed any offensive intentions by his government, this success caused many in Tehran to focus their attention upon the Shi'a holy city of Karbala, only 80 kilometres south of Baghdad – or even advancing all the way to Jerusalem.[61]

Fatah al-Mobin enabled the IRGC to launch a diversionary attack against the new defences of IV Corps' southern flank, during 30 March – 1 April, in support of the great Iranian offensive in Khuzestan – Operation Beit-ol-Mogaddas.[62] This attack resulted in the Pasdaran pushing through positions of 34th Armoured and 606th Infantry Brigades in direction of Fakkeh, before being stopped by the corps commando battalion. The IRGC then launched a new attack from the south, during the night of 5 – 6 May, broke through, inflicted heavy casualties upon 34th and 51st Armoured, 27th Mechanized and 426th Infantry Brigades, before reaching the international border. However, the Iraqis held onto Fakkeh.[63]

Ultimately, the Iranian victories at Khorammshar and east of Fakkeh caused Saddam to surrender most of his ill-gotten gains from 1980. The II Corps was forced to abandon Qasr-e Shirin, Sumar, and Mehran to withdraw to better defensive positions inside Iraq. Shortly afterwards, partially because of the failure of the first Iranian attempt to take Basra (Operation Ramadan Mubarak), the corps then found itself exposed to probes against its 14th Infantry Division on 6 August, and its 12th Armoured Division on 8 August 1982.[64]

Operation Moslem Ibn Akil

Following the bloody disaster of Ramadan Mubarrak, the Iranian SDC met in mid-August 1982 to discuss its next move. This time, the clerics were more amenable to the JCS' suggestions about striking a more exposed section of the front and selected positions opposite Sumar. These were based upon the 320-400-metre-high Haran Hills, straddling the border and pierced by the River Gangir (Kangir). This area was dominated by Mandali – a major communication hub, linked by a hard-topped road to Baqubah, some 45 kilometres further west, and then to Baghdad, only 120 kilometres away. Mandali also controlled a network of minor roads along the frontier and across the northern marshes, 50 kilometres east of Baqubah, and to the HQ of II Corps in Mansouriyah.

The area was garrisoned by 12th Armoured Division (Brigadier-General Shawkat Ahmed Atta), who knew the Iranians had begun assembling forces around Sumar but was uncertain about their

A dramatic photograph taken during one of many ad hoc infantry charges by IRGC's volunteers, sometime in 1982. While often initiated by little else but frustration and giving birth to the legends about 'human wave tactics' early on, over time the Pasdaran learned how to direct and control such attacks – and the Iraqis learned to fear them. (Tom Cooper Collection)

An Iranian soldier with a 9M14 Malyutka (AT-3 Sagger) ATGM. Large numbers of such missiles were deployed by Iranian military starting in 1982. Some were captured from Iraqi stocks, while others were imported via Syria and Libya. (via N. S.)

Operation Fatah al-Mobin was one of most successful Iranian offensives of the Iran-Iraq War. It resulted in the capture of dozens of thousands of Iraqi troops and hundreds of armoured vehicles. This Iranian guard is watching over several hundreds of Iraqi prisoners of war in March 1982 (Albert Grandolini Collection)

intentions. Saddam is known to have visited Baqubah on 12 September, but without any useful results.

Commanded by Colonel A. Rostami, the Iranian forces involved in the operation named Moslem Ibn Akil (after the martyred cousin of Imams Hassan and Hussain) included the 4th Brigade of 81st Armoured Division IRIA, part of 55th Airborne Brigade, 27th Mohammad Rasoolallah and 31st Ashura Divisions IRGC, and 18th al-Ghadir and 21st Imam Reza Brigades IRGC – for a total of 33,000 troops, supported by 50 MBTs and 100 guns. The IRIAF prepared all F-4Es of TFB.3 for this operation, while the IRIAA forward deployed one of its Combat Support Groups.[65]

Fire in the Hills
Although the defenders were alert, the attackers exploited the terrain to infiltrate enemy positions at 18 points along a 35-kilometre-wide front on the Haran Hills during the night of 30 September – 1 October 1982, and then push on for up to two kilometres. Reinforced by brigades from 7th Infantry Division, Shawkat Ahmed Atta counterattacked and regained the terrain, but the Iranians attacked again during the following night and punched through, reaching the heights on both sides of the river. Counter-attacks by 37th Armoured Division and 46th Mechanised Brigades prevented further advances, and left the Iranians with a meagre booty of about 110 prisoners and a dozen of tanks.

Nevertheless, Rostami regrouped his forces and attacked again during the night of 5 – 6 October, this time reaching suburbs of

Mandali. Somewhat shaken, the Iraqis counter-attacked on 10 November, using the new 17th Armoured Division's 59th and 70th Armoured Brigades, and Atta's 50th Armoured Brigade, plus four squadrons of IrAAC to push the enemy 10 kilometres away from Mandali.

A week later, 81st Infantry Division IRIA spearheaded a renewed attack, but this was stopped by well-prepared Iraqi artillery and multiple counterattacks. Ultimately, the Iranian forces claimed the capture of 12 AFVs and 20 artillery pieces, while IRIAA's gunships were credited with destruction of 25 AFVs. While successful in defense the Iraqis had little to show, but issued obscure claims to the foreign press, for example, that one of their 'Mi-24' helicopters had shot down an IRIAF F-4 Phantom II using a Soviet-made AT-6 anti-tank guided missile (ATGM).[66]

Operation Moharram al-Haram
Muslim Ibn Akil fanned the embers of tensions between the IRIA and the IRGC, leading to bitter arguments over tactics. The professional Iranian officers accused the militias of poor training and slapdash style of fighting, while the Pasdaran complained about the lack of revolutionary zeal among the military leadership. Eventually, Speaker of the Iranian Parliament (and future President of the IRI), Akbar Hashemi Rafsanjani, announced that the new Iranian policy would be to, 'hit the enemy with restricted blows'.[67]

A corresponding offensive was then planned for the area south of Dehloran, with the intention of eliminating the Iraqi-controlled enclave around Musiyan (Musian) and obtaining a bridgehead for advance on Amarah during the holy month of Muharram. Hence, the operation in question was named Muharram al-Harram (Holy Muharram). The SDC may have had a political motive for the operation because the captured terrain might later win concessions at the negotiating table. To execute the attack it transferred two brigades of 21st Infantry Division IRIA, together with 25th Karbala and 30th Beit-ol-Moghaddas Divisions IRGC, from the south. These helped establish the Task Force Zafar, which consisted of one armoured and four infantry divisions, two brigades of Pasdaran, and two IRIA infantry brigades, for a total of 51,000 troops (including about 9,000 regulars). The IRIA provided support in the form of 51 artillery- and 2 MRLS-batteries (300 artillery pieces), and five tank battalions (with M60s and Chieftains), while the IRIAA added 46 helicopters (including 16 AH-1Js, of which eight were armed with

Iranians collecting Iraqi troops captured during the Operation Moslem Ibn Akil. (Tom Cooper Colection)

A BRDM-2 armoured reconnaissance car equipped with six launchers for 9P133 Malyutka (AT-3 Sagger) ATGMs, was one of hundreds of Iraqi vehicles captured by the Iranians during the first half of 1982. As indicated by its insignia, it was subsequently pressed into service with the IRGC. (Albert Grandolini Collection)

BGM-71 TOW ATGMs). For further details on involved units, see Table 3.

The northern prong of this offensive aimed to cross the frontier and take the road hub at Tib, and the nearby high terrain. The southern prong was to cross the border and capture the ridge north of Abu Ghirab (Abu-Qarrab or Abu Ghorab).

Facing them on a 50-kilometre front was IV Corps of the Iraqi Army, including 10th Armoured Division (Major-General Thabit Sultan Ahmed) on the left, facing Musiyan; 20th Infantry Division (Brigadier-General Farouk Twafiq Abdur Razak) on the right; while Fakkeh was shielded by 1st Mechanized Division. Primary defence positions consisted of two lines of mutually-supporting strongpoints running along a river bank, which – combined with minefields, ravines and water courses – were expected to channel the attackers into killing zones. Infantry was deployed forward, and expected to fall back under pressure along pre-planned lines; drawing the enemy into open areas where armour could counter-attack. This force totalled about 48,000 troops, 340 MBTs and 180 artillery pieces on the Musiyan front, and some 34,000 troops, 380 MBTs and 150 artillery pieces on the Fakkeh front.[68]

Table 3: Order of Battle for Operation Muharram al-Harram, 1982

Corps	Division	Brigades
Iran		
Task Force Zafar	21st Infantry Division IRIA	1st Brigade
	77th Infantry Division IRIA	3 brigades
	84th Infantry Brigade IRIA	
	8th Najaf Ashraf Infantry Division IRGC	3 brigades
	14th Imam Hossein Infantry Division IRGC	3 brigades
	17th Ali Ibn Abu Talib Infantry Division IRGC	3 brigades
	25th Karbala Infantry Division IRGC	3 brigades
	30th Beit-ol-Moghaddas Armoured Division IRGC	3 brigades
	35th Imam Hassan Infantry Brigade IRGC	
	44th Qamar Bani Hashem Engineer Brigade IRGC	
	33rd Artillery Group IRIA	
	44th Artillery Group IRIA	
	1st & 4th CSG IRIAA	
Iraq		
IV Corps	Corps troops, including IV Corps Artillery Brigade	
	1st Mechanised Division	34th & 51st Armoured Brigades; 1st & 27th Mechanised Brigade; 93rd, 96th, 109th & 426th Infantry Brigades
	10th Armoured Division	17th & 42nd Armoured Brigades; 24th Mechanised Brigade; 423rd, 501st, 606th & 701st Infantry Brigades
	20th Infantry Division	44th, 420th & 435th Infantry Brigades

Fighting in the Rain

The Pasdaran opened their assault in heavy rain during the night of 31 October – 1 November 1982. The Najaf Ashraf and Karbala Divisions advanced on the right of the 30-kilometre wide frontline, while Ali Ibn Abu Talib and Imam Hossein Divisions pushed on the left. The defences collapsed under the onslaught, and the Iranians drove forward for 5-8 kilometres, taking Tib and the Bayat oilfield in the process. Thabit Sultan launched his well-rehearsed counter-attack during the afternoon of 2 November, but this became bogged down in mud, and resulted only in the recovery of Tib. In the south, Muharram opened badly as the attackers ran into an extensive minefield that inflicted crippling casualties and ended the attack almost as soon as it began.

The Iranians continued attacking on 4, 6, and 8 November, expanding their bridgehead by taking more of the high ground. The IRIAA is known to have carried 2,194 troops and 85 tonnes of supplies to the frontlines, while evacuating 1,521 wounded. Its TOW-equipped Cobras reportedly destroyed 107 enemy vehicles.

However, Fakhri's new 60th Armoured Brigade and commandos helped contain their further breakthroughs. Finally, the Iraqis launched an all-out counterattack on the night of 9-10 November, and regained some of the lost ground within the following 15 hours, before their counterattack was virtually washed away by rain. Eventually the Iranians managed an advance of up to 10 kilometres deep into Iraq, and regained about 440 square kilometres of their own territory. Tehran subsequently claimed the capture of 3,000-3,500 enemy troops and 14 MBTs (including 9 T-55s), but the operation clearly failed to reach its objectives. Still, for the clerics, Fatah al-Mobbin and Muharram 'demonstrated the best way forward' and strongly influenced the operations of the year 1983.[69]

Val Fajr Moghaddamati

Despite the disappointment of 'Muharram' on the Fakkeh front, in early 1983 the SDC demanded a new assault to outflank the Doveyrich line, take Fakkeh and then, in a surfeit of ambition, to advance along a minor road across the marshes to Amarah. Dubbed Val Fajr Moghaddamati (Dawn Prelude) this eventually became the first of a series of operations code-named Val Fajr (Dawn).[70]

Commanded by Colonel Mohammed Baqeri, the Iranian forces were concentrated for an attack from north and south towards Fakkeh, and included two Task Forces: Karbala and Najaf. These included four divisions of the IRGC, two brigades of 16th Armoured Division IRIA, and 84th Infantry Brigade, as well as detachments from 21st Infantry Division, 23rd Special Forces and 55th Airborne Brigades. The concentration totalled some 60,000 troops (including 25,000 from IRIA), and was supported by 200 MBTs, 58 helicopters (including 18 AH-1s), and 33rd and 55th Artillery Groups IRIA (21 batteries, of which 12 were self-propelled) with 150 guns.

Fought in an area of sandy desert dunes northwest of Bostan, this battle would be the baptism of fire for the 18th Infantry Division (commanded by Brigadier-General Hashim Ahmed), which held a 15-kilometre line around Al-Shib (Sheeb). This was a large formation, including three brigades (95th, 702nd, and 704th Infantry), with 15,000 troops, 72 guns and 18 BM-21 MRLS. Furthermore, the Iraqi COMINT had alerted the defenders, which resulted in the re-deployment of Brigadier-General Hussein Rashid Muhammad's 3rd Armoured Division, together with 36th Infantry, 65th and 68th Special Forces Brigades. Finally, the GHQ added 49th and 108th Infantry Brigades. All of the Iraqi artillery in this area was put under the command of the corps artillery brigade, together with most of 1st Mechanized Division's artillery.[71]

The Iranians opened their attack in heavy rain just before midnight on 6-7 February 1983, with Karbala's Saheb az-Zaman and Vali Asr Division probing across the dunes south of Fakkeh, into a sector held by 702nd and 704th Infantry Brigades. Well-constructed and extensive defences easily held off the attacks, but the Iranians re-launched their assault in the morning and their spearheads reached the road connecting Fakkeh with Shib before they were driven back by 12th Armoured Brigade of 3rd Armoured Division.

Fakhri's centralisation of his artillery paid dividends and his gunners inflicted heavy losses, especially among the Basiji, while the IRIA's failure to assemble an adequate stock of shells limited their preparation and counter-battery fire. When Iranian pressure became too great, Fakhri's troops were deliberately withdrawn to entice the enemy forward and expose them to mechanised counter-attacks, involving up to three brigades which drove back the enemy.

Obviously failing to learn the lesson of reinforcing success rather than failure, the Iranians rushed in reinforcements of one armoured and six infantry brigades, and attacked again during the night of 7 – 8

February. This time they did manage to cut the Fakkeh-Shib road, despite heavy air strikes in the course of which the IrAF deployed its new Dassault Mirage F.1EQ fighter-bombers for the first time, while IrAAC helicopters flew up to 150 sorties a day. By contrast the IRIAF played next to no part in this operation.

When his third attack failed, and struggling to regain the initiative, Baqeri then committed two brigades of 16th Armoured Division IRIA on a 1.5 kilometres wide front, starting on the afternoon of 9 February 1983. These ground their way through Iraqi positions, and beat back a counterattack of 12th Armoured Brigade. However, when the dawn broke, they found themselves exposed and unsupported in an open plain. Whether due to incompetence of the IRIA staff, or Pasdaran failure, this provided the Iraqis with a splendid opportunity for a corps-sized counterattack. Spearheaded by 3rd Armoured Division and 1st Mechanized Brigade of the Republican Guards, this saw 250 Iraqi MBTs sweeping along the frontier from the northwest before smashing into Iranian ranks, leaving up to 100 MBTs and 80 APCs knocked out or abandoned intact in its trail.

Val Fajr Moghaddamati thus ended with a defeat and then the usual – bloody – bickering before the Iranians realised they couldn't gain anything, and went onto defensive on 17 February 1983. By then, the Iranians had suffered 8,000 casualties – including about 1,000 prisoners of war – while the Iraqis lost about 6,000.[72]

Val Fajr-1

Despite the failure of Val Fajr Moghaddamati, Rafsanjani persuaded the SDC to launch a new attack; Valr Fajr-1. This used the same task forces, but reinforced to more than 100,000 troops (including 40,000 from IRIA), nearly 200 MBTs, and more than 300 artillery pieces, as outlined in Table 3. The IRIA added 31 helicopters (including 9 AH-1s). Crucial Iraqi units remained 10th Armoured Division and 20th Infantry Division, commanded by Thabit Sultan Ahmed and Farouk Tawfiq Abdur Razzak, respectively, while 1st Mechanized Division continued to shield Fakkeh.[73]

The Iranian assault began during the night of 10 – 11 April 1983, with Task Force Najaf attacking on a 32-kilometre wide front against 20th Infantry Division. Despite heavy casualties, the Pasdaran punched through the position of 60th Armoured Brigade and 501st Infantry Brigade, and then drove for 20 kilometres deep into Iraq. Early in the morning of 11 April, the Iraqis launched a divisional counter-attack, spearheaded by 42nd Armoured Brigade. However, they regained only the southern part of the lost terrain. Nevertheless, the Task Force Najaf was thus out of steam and its offensive over.

Further south, Task Force Karbala penetrated the positions of 51st Armoured and 108th Infantry Brigades, aided by hand-to-hand fighting. To prevent the collapse of their frontline, the Iraqis deployed the 65th Special Forces Brigade as 1st Mechanized Division and 34th Armoured Brigade launched a counter-attack supported by 87 attack sorties of the IrAF. However, this effort failed to regain the lost positions. Fakhri now decided to concentrate his forces and co-ordinate all of their operations with that of the newly-arrived 3rd Armoured Division (commanded by Hussein Rashid Muhammad), which now controlled 10 brigades.

Supported by another 150 attack sorties of the IrAF, and heavy artillery support, this counter-attack was launched on 15 April and saw the Iranians withdrawing after only a few hours – their AH-1s claimed destruction of up to 56 AFVs, whilst losing a third of their number to Iraqi air defences. Certainly enough, the Iraqis took another two days of mopping up to regain all of their positions (and

Iranian offensives on the central front of late 1982 often saw intensive deployment of IRIAA's helicopters. Here a typical formation of Bell 214As is seen passing one of the local mountain peaks. (Farzin Nadimi Collection)

Despite significant success during earlier fighting, by 1983 the Iranian air force began showing clear signs of exhaustion. Because of this, and because of growing strength of the Iraqi Air Force, ground-based means of air defence – like this IRGC-operated ZSU-23-4 Shilka self-propelled flak – became ever more important for the defence of the battlefield. (via N. S.)

collect about 1,000 prisoners), but Val Fajr-1 was over by 17 April 1983. US Intelligence estimated the Iraqis suffered 6,000-8,000 casualties and the Iranians 15,000. Shortly afterwards, Rafsanjani indicated that his country's losses were too high and that in future greater care should be taken to prevent unnecessary losses.

Table 4: Order of Battle for Val Fajr-1, April 1983

Corps	Division	Brigades
Iran		
Task Force Najaf	77th Infantry Division IRIA	2nd Brigade only
	37th Armoured Brigade IRIA	1 battalion only
	55th Airborne Brigade IRIA	
	58th infantry Brigade IRIA	
	84th Infantry Brigade IRIA	
	5th Nasr Infantry Division IRGC	1 brigade
	11th Amir al-Momenim Infantry Division IRGC	
	19th Fajr Infantry Division IRGC	1 brigade
	27th Mohammad Rasoolallah Infantry Division IRGC	1 brigade
	31st Ashura Infantry Division IRGC	1 brigade
Task Force Karbala	21st Infantry Division IRIA	2nd and 3rd Brigades
	7th Vali Asr Infantry Division IRGC	1 brigade
	8th Najaf Ashraf Infantry Division IRGC	1 brigade
	41st Sarallah Infantry Brigade IRGC	
	55th Artillery Group IRIA	
Iraq		
II Corps	65th and 66th Commando brigades, II Corps Artillery Brigade	
	1st Mechanised Division	34th & 51st Armoured Brigades;, 1st & 27th Mechanised Brigades;, 108th Infantry Brigade
	3rd Armoured Division	6th, & 12th Armoured Brigades; 8th Mechanised Brigade
	10th Armoured Division	17th & 42nd Armoured Brigades; 24th Mechanised Brigade; 38th, 48th Infantry Brigades
	20th Infantry Division	60th Armoured Brigade; 44th, 420th, 435th & 501st Infantry Brigades

Val Fajr-3

Undaunted by this failure, the SDC prepared their next offensive – Val Fajr-3 (for Val Fajr-2, see next chapter). This was to be undertaken further north, with the aim of eliminating an Iraqi-held enclave that remained after the abandonment of Mehran, in May 1982. Mehran lies in the broad east-to-west valley of the River Gawi; this is only some 30 metres wide with its southern boundary sharply defined by a steep escarpment of the Jebal Hamrin/Khur-e Khurmaleh. The northern part consists of the Kamar Charmak mountains, that are up to 1,290 metres high and are cut by the Kunjan Pass through which flows the River Galal Badra, a subsidiary of the Gawi. A cultivated area extends for some 10 kilometres north of the town to the border, with a narrower band on the southern banks of the Gawi extending another 10 kilometres.

The north-eastern approaches to the town are via a web of streams and irrigation canals across which the main highway to Kermanshah runs. Further east this road then runs up the Gavi Valley, before crossing an escarpment. Some 10 kilometres north of Mehran there is a crossroads with one road running westwards across the border to Badrah through Zurbatiyah (Zorbaitiyah). A second road bypasses Mehran to link up with the highway some 15 kilometres east of Mehran. The town itself is only some 80 kilometres north of the Baghdad-Basra highway at al-Kut. Indeed, the IRGC's garrison of Mehran was in peril because of its proximity to major roads inside Iraq.

For their attack, the Pasdaran assembled the reduced 5th Nasr- and reinforced part of 41st Sarallah-, together with brigades from 11th Amir all-Momenin, 17th Ali Ibn Abu Talib, 21st Imam Reza, and 40th Sarab Divisions, plus a battalion from 27th Mohammad Rasoolallah Division IRGC. Supported by 4th Armoured Brigade of 21st Division IRIA, and a battalion from 84th Infantry Brigade, the forces involved totalled about 35,000 troops.

Mehran was the bailiwick of II Corps under Lieutenant-General Mohammed Fathi Amin (transferred from I Corps); the 2nd and 22nd Infantry Divisions had established strong defences along the western edge of the irrigated area, and then in an arc west of Mehran. The GMID was aware of the enemy build-up but concluded the Iranian attack would be launched north of Zurbatiyah. To make sure, Baghdad boosted Amin's reserved with 1st and 2nd Brigades of the Guards Corps, and also launched a pre-emptive attack by two mechanized brigades on 29 July 1983 in vain.[74]

However, their hopes were soon dashed, for the Iranians struck out of the Mehran area during the night of 29 – 30 July and in a new fashion; with armour in the lead. The Pasdaran infantry meanwhile encircled and isolated a battalion of 417th Infantry Brigade: positioned high in the hills, this unit was usually supplied by helicopters only. It was authorised to break out during the night of 8 – 9 August 1983. The Iranians were also successful against 2nd Infantry Brigade, and an attempt by the Iraqi 38th Infantry Brigade to help was so badly handled that its commander was subsequently executed for incompetence – although his ATGM-teams managed to hold enemy tanks. The next day, supported by multiple strikes of F-4Es from TFB.3, the Iranians pushed the enemy across the border and occupied most of the Kulak-i-Buzurg, while taking about 400 prisoners. The Iraqis also employed their air power; with up to 150 attack sorties on 31 July alone.

Fathi Amin organized a corps counter-attack on 2 August, deploying both Guards' brigades, together with corps commandos, and elements from his own 7th Infantry-, 12th Armoured and 17th Armoured Divisions. While recovering much of the lost territory, this effort was eventually abandoned on 4 August 1983.

With Saddam demanding the recovery of Mehran, Amin reorganized his troops and attacked again during the night of 5 – 6 August 1983. This time, 8th Mechanized and 12th Armoured Brigade of 3rd Armoured Division, and 48th Infantry Brigade set out to isolate the town from the north, while the reinforced 70th Armoured Brigade (17th Armoured Division) pushed from the south. After encountering fierce resistance, both attempts were abandoned on 9 August. Meanwhile the Iranians began pushing into Iraq in the south towards Zurbatiyah, but were stopped outside the town by Iraqi reinforcements hurriedly withdrawn from their counterattack, the Iranians, however, still managed to secure Kulak-i-Buzurg.

By the time both sides stopped combat operations Iraqi casualties were estimated at 10,000-17,000; Tehran claimed victory although suffering between 15,000 and 25,000 killed or injured. Some Iranian casualties were caused by chemical weapons deployed by the IrAF during this offensive, however, such operations had little effect due to failure to allow for wind conditions. The Iraqis also deployed the mustard gas, which was heavier than air and tended to roll down the heights away from Iranian positions.

Val Fajr-5 and Val Fajr-6

With neither side undertaking any major operations on this sector of the border for the rest of 1983, it was only in February of the following year that the Central Front became active again. However, operations Val Fajr-5 and Val Fajr-6 were diversionary attacks against the positions of II and IV Corps, intended to draw Iraqi attention away from the actual big offensive – Operation Khaiber.[75] Val Fajr-5 was launched on the night of 15 – 16 February 1984, with two IRGC divisions attacking the well-entrenched 2nd Infantry Division on the right flank of II Corps. While highly successful in using dry river beds to infiltrate enemy defences, the Pasdaran were subsequently cut to pieces by artillery and air power, followed by a counterattack by the 12th Armoured Division, launched during the night of 19 – 20 February.

Val Fajr-6 exploited dense fog when three IRGC divisions (18th al-Ghadir, 25th Karbala and 105th Qods) struck the newly-established 25th Infantry Division, on the northern side of IV Corps, during the night of 21 – 22 February 1984. Although storming numerous positions and isolating others, the Iranians were then struck heavily by a counterattack from 24th Mechanized and 42nd Armoured Brigades of 10th Armoured Division, and the following night lost all the ground they had gained. The IRGC's southern attempt aimed at Al-Shib was an even briefer affair, and only offered the units of the Iraqi Popular Army an opportunity to distinguish themselves.[76]

'Quiet' Years

With both sides busy fighting big battles in the Hawizeh Marshes, the spring and summer were quiet; in September 1984, however, the Iranian CFOHQ was sharply criticised by everyone from the IRIA to the local gendarmerie over the security of the border between Ilam and Dehloran where there had been numerous ambushes by Iraqi Special Forces. Therefore, on 30 September 1984, decision was taken to launch Operaiton Ashura – or Val Fajr-7 – against a 20-kilometre front of Iraqi bridgehead on the Meimak Heights, west of Salehabad.

Assembled under Task Force Najaf, the assault group consisted of 1st and 3rd Brigades of the 81st Division IRIA, 84th Infantry Division, and a brigade each of 5th Nasr, 21st Imam Reza, and 32nd Ansar al-Hossein Divisions, and the 29th Nabi-y Akram Brigade IRGC. During the night of 17 – 18 October 1984, the Iranians infiltrated positions of II Iraqi Corps around Saif Saad all the way to their artillery emplacements. However, stubborn defence by 22nd Infantry Division and a counterattack by elements of 12th Armoured Division quickly secured the situation. Another Iranian attack, launched on 20 October, overran a battalion of 4th Infantry Brigade, resulting in the loss of some heights west of the border road.

By coincidence, only a day earlier, Saddam and new Army Chief-of-Staff, Lieutenant-General Abd al-Jawad Dhanun, paid a two-day visit to the corps and authorised the deployment of the newly-established Hammurabi Guards Armoured Division to the II Corps' area. On 22 October this unit launched a counter-attack, but despite strong air and artillery support failed to regain all of the lost ground and called off their attack. As Cordsman noted, this kind of Iranian attack posed serious problems for the Iraqis for it meant that Iraq had "...the alternative of either ceding the loss or counterattacking and sustaining casualties for relatively unimportant objectives."[77]

The Central Front remained quiet in 1985, with both sides conducting only minor raids to improve their positions, or disturb the enemy. Most related Iraqi operations were a part of Saddam's 'dynamic defence policy'. They began with 606th Infantry Brigade (16th Infantry Division) taking key heights north of the Mandali-Sumar road, on the night of 30 – 31 January 1985, to prevent the Iranians from shelling nearby Iraqi towns and villages. A more ambitious operation resulted in the capture of heights in the Mehran sector, during the night of 11 – 12 February, by 2nd Infantry Division and commandos; and 434th Infantry Brigade (12th Armoured Division) in the Saif Saad sector. Similar raids were launched by II Corps during July and August. The IV Corps launched such raids in February, July, and September 1985.[78]

The Iranians launched several raids of their own, primarily against II Corps around Qasr-e Shirin (Operations Zafar-1 and Zafar-3, Qods-1 and Qods-2, all undertaken in June 1985, and followed by Qods-5 in August). However, their largest attack was Operation Ashura-2, which struck 114th Infantry Brigade of 37th Armoured Division on 15 August, and Ashura-3, which hit 108th Infantry Brigade of 1st Mechanized Division, in Fakkeh sector only

a day later. Qods-3 followed in July, Qods-4 in early August, and Ashura-4 in October 1985. While inflicting casualties and gaining some ground, none of these enterprises was of any great significance.

Following a winter lull, raiding was resumed on the night of 6 – 7 April 1986, when IV Corps struck the Tib sector. Two days later, part of 1st Mechanized Division launched a similar mission in the Doveyrich River Valley, while on 13 April, 29th Infantry Division raided enemy bases in the Hawizah Marshes. Larger operations followed on 30 April, when 1st Mechanized and 10th Armoured Divisions took an area 12 kilometres deep and 21 kilometres wide in the Fakkeh-Chenaneh sector, and repelled a counter-attack by 16th IRIA Armoured Division, launched during the night of 2 – 3 May. There was a similar attack during the night of 8 – 9 May, when 1st Mechanized and 20th Infantry Divisions captured a 100-square-kilometre sector in Doveyrich Valley, despite a counterattack by the IRGC supported by IRIAA Cobras.[79] Some of the raids may have been intended as diversions, prompted by Iraq's loss of the Faw Peninsula during Operation Val Fajr-8 in February 1986. The loss of this critical piece of terrain – and the failure to regain it – undermined Saddam's political ambitions and hurt his prestige both at home and abroad. Saddam's gaze thus fell on Mehran – lost during Val Fajr-3, which, he believed, might prove a useful bargaining chip in exchange for Faw. Furthermore, in the light of repeated Iranian announcements of another 'final' offensive for 19 May 1986 (the anniversary of the death of Ali, Prophet Mohammed's nephew), he feared that the Iranians might use Mehran for a large-scale attack across the Tigris River.

Heroes' Revenge

The task of regaining Mehran – Operation Heroes' Revenge – fell upon Lieutenant-General Zia Tawfik Ibrahim's II Corps. Tawfik actually feared he would be exposed to a repeat of Val Fajr-3 over the same terrain, and would have preferred to strike further south towards Dehloran, where he might take high ground which was easier to hold. However, he was overruled and delegated the planning to his Chief-of-Staff, Brigadier-General Ayad Khlil Zaki, who dusted off the plans to regain Mehran developed after Val

Long columns of IRGC combatants on the march during Operation Val Fajr-5, in the Mehran area, February 1984. (IRGC)

One of the Iranian strongpoints on a dominating peak – in this case the 'Hill 402' – of the northern frontlines. (IRIA)

Fajr-3. Zaki intended to envelop the town from the north with 4th Commando, 49th Armoured, and 94th Infantry Brigades under his personal command, and from the south by a force consisting of 5th Commando, 70th Armoured, and 417th Infantry Brigades commanded by Brigadier-General Nawfal Ismail Hammadi. The GHQ's 606th Infantry Brigade acted as reserve. These units totalled some 25,000 troops, supported by 250 MBTs. They faced about 10,000 defenders from a brigade each of 21st and 84th Divisions IRIA.[80]

Tawfik's troops moved out on the evening of 16 May 1986. Zaki's northern force quickly pushed 4th Brigade of 21st Infantry Division back, and secured the high ground by 18 May. Ismail's tube and rocket artillery inflicted heavy casualties upon 84th IRIA Division, which was manning nine 4-metre-high berms across the valley, and broke through to reach the town by dusk on 17 May. There followed two days of bitter street fighting, by the end of which the Iraqis had established a 15-kilometre deep bridgehead of 160 square kilometres inside Iran. This was protected in the north by the peaks around Reza Abad, overlooking the town and covering the northern crossroads. However, the Iraqi advance up the Gawi Valley was held some 3-4 kilometres short of the eastern road junction, leaving the Iranians in control of communications from the east. This was to prove a serious mistake.[81]

Karbala-1

Saddam's offer to exchange Mehran for Faw was brusquely rejected by Tehran, which almost instantly ordered its military into a counterattack. Probing operations had already begun on the morning of 19 May, notably in the north, where a brigade of 5th Nasr Infantry Division IRGC struck 59th Armoured Brigade in the Kunjan Dam area. The Iraqi positions held, but Tawfik's armour-heavy force was unable to push into the nearby heights to prevent the Iranians from assembling larger forces there. During the following six weeks, the Iranians rushed to prepare Operation Karbala-1. For this purpose, Task Force Najaf was re-deployed to this area, and filled with about 20,000 Pasdaran and Basiji from numerous local units. Several IRIA units – including 44th Artillery Group – followed, totalling about 12,000 troops, 100 MBTs and 37 helicopters (including 10 AH-1s; for further details on involved units, see Table 5).

Meanwhile, Nawfal Ismail's 17th Armoured Division was given responsibility for the salient, but he fell ill and his replacement restricted all patrols to within 20 kilometres of Mehran, thus hindering chances of detecting Iranian preparations.[82] The northern front of the salient was held by 417th and 443rd Infantry Brigades, while 425th and 705th Infantry Brigades entrenched themselves in

the east. 59th and 70th Armoured Brigades were held in reserve. Overall, the garrison totalled some 22,000 troops, supported by around 180 MBTs.

The 17th Armoured Division found itself under fierce pressure from 10 June 1986. Tawfiq requested air support, but because Saddam forbade direct requests to the IrAF, these were delayed, and the few fighter-bombers which did appear proved ineffective. Moreover, Saddam seems to have had second thoughts about holding Mehran, and reportedly decided to abandon the town on 30 June. Consequently, the assembly of the Iranian assault forces not only proceeded unhindered but also largely undetected.[83]

Whether or not Saddam's decision to abandon Mehran was communicated to local commanders became purely academic, as during the night of 30 June – 1 July 1986, the Seyed o-Shohada, Ali Ibn Abu Talib, Karbala, and Mohammad IRGC Infantry Divisions struck the positions of 443rd and 705th Infantry Brigades around Hill 233, east of Reza Abad. The defenders resisted tenaciously, but lost heavily and conducted a fighting withdrawal, covered by armour. The famous commander of 70th Armoured Brigade, Colonel Jawhar Kalil – nicknamed 'The Wolf' – was killed while leading a counter-attack. Similarly, 100 air strikes by IrAF, and 33 by IrAAC, as well as deployment of the 65th Special Forces and 606th Infantry Brigades from the reserve, were in vain: by 2 July, the Iraqis were forced back, almost to the border. It was only during the second phase of Karbala-1 – launched on 4 July with the aim of pushing westwards into Iraq – that the Iranian assault was finally stopped. The Iraqis suffered about 3,000 casualties (including more than 1,000 prisoners) leading Saddam to relieve Tawfik and replace him with Lieutenant-General Abd as-Sattar Ahmed al-Muaini.[84]

Table 5: Order of Battle for Karbala-1, May 1986

Corps	Division	Brigades
Iran		
Task Force Najaf	5th Nasr Infantry Division IRGC	1 brigade
	10th Seyed o-Shohada Infantry Division IRGC	1 brigade
	17th Ali Ibn Abu Talib Infantry Division IRGC	1 brigade
	25th Karbala Infantry Division IRGC	1 brigade
	27th Mohammad Infantry Division IRGC	2 brigades
	41st Sarallah Infantry Division IRGC	1 brigade
	15th Imam Hassan Infantry Brigade IRGC	
	21st Imam Reza Infantry Brigade IRGC	
	662nd Beit-ol-Moghaddas Infantry Brigade IRGC	
	84th Infantry Division IRIA	1 brigade
	44th Artillery Group IRIA	
	1st & 2nd CSG IRIAA, 4th GSG IRIA	
Iraq		
II Corps	65th Commando Brigade, II Corps Artillery Brigade	

		59th & 70th Armoured Brigades; 417th, 425th, 443rd & 705th Infantry Brigades
	17th Armoured Division	
Reserves	606th Infantry Brigade	
	2nd Wing IrAAC	

Iranian troops inside one of the Iraqi positions captured during the Operation Karabala-6 in January 1987. (Albert Grandolini Collection)

Shirazi conferring with several commanders at one of IRIAA's forward bases. Notable are three AH-1J Cobras and a single Bell 206 in the background. (Tom Cooper Collection)

Lacking replacements for earlier tank losses, the IRIA was forced to keep its obsolete M47 Patton MBTs in service with the 77th Infantry Division throughout the war. (via N. S.)

Crisis of Morale

The failure to regain the Faw Peninsula, followed by the loss of Mehran, caused a major crisis in the morale of the Iraqi armed forces. However, it also acted as a catalyst for radical reforms which had been needed for years. The generals' muted grumbling about Saddam's meddling in military issues increased when the Iranians exploited their earlier success to capture additional heights west of Mehran, during the night of 16 – 17 September 1986. This time it took the deployment of 94th and 118th Infantry Brigades of the new I Special Corps to stabilise the situation.[85] Eventually, Saddam was forced to call an Extraordinary Congress of the Ba'ath Party. Little has emerged about the deliberations, but the Iraqis did decide to introduce major changes in recruitment and strategy. Now the army would conscript more officers from university students to improve the overall quality, while their generals would adopt a more active strategy. Progress was certainly made, but it was given real momentum by Khazraji's appointment as Chief-of-Staff, in 1987.[86]

Meanwhile, raiding continued, but on 14 October 1986, the Iranians struck II Corps at Qasr-e Shirin again, pushing 21st Infantry Division off several key heights. This time, it took an intervention by 68th Special Forces Brigade and a corps commando battalion to recover the ground.[87]

Karbala-6

During the latter half of 1986 the SDC was pre-occupied with preparing its 'war-winning offensives' on Basra; Karbala-4 and -5. However, diversions were planned to support these operations; and the SDC came to the decision to launch a diversion, Operation Karbala-6, in early 1987, to regain Naft Shahr, northwest of Sumar, and thus remove one of the burrs in Iran's skin.

Naft Shahr lies near the border, on the northern bank of the Kanga Kush, across the Khanaqin-Sumar road – at the mouth of a gently sloping river valley to the east and a narrow gorge to the

Iranian army troops carrying an injured comrade on a makeshift 'stretcher' made of two FN-FAL assault rifles. (Albert Grandolini Collection)

north. The Iraqis held the eastern side of the gorge, and a line due south to the point where the salient protruded into Iraq. This road went around the western base of a height, and control of that height and the road would provide a valuable springboard for an assault upon Al Miqdadiyah, but it was poor tank country. With most of the IRGC's units busy fighting for Basra, Karbala-6 was one of the rare IRIA-led operations from this period of the war. The army deployed 2nd and 3rd Brigades of 21st Infantry Division, 3rd Brigade of 77th Infantry Division, an unknown brigade of 84th Infantry division, elements of 58th Infantry Division and 55th Airborne Brigade.

The IRGC-element was confined to two brigades of 31st Ashura Infantry Division, reinforced by several battalions of Basiji. Overall, the Iranians concentrated about 30,000 troops, supported by one tank- and 17 artillery battalions (about 185 guns and MRLs). They faced 16th and 22nd Infantry Divisions commanded by Brigadiers Abd Mutlak al-Juburi and Tariq Radi Hassan, respectively, who had six brigades with about 19,000 troops.

Bad weather forced several postponements and helped alert the defenders. Once the assault began, during the night of 13 – 14 January 1987, Iraqi defences channelled the attackers, spearheaded by the 77th Division's brigade and Ashura's Pasdaran (supported by few captured Iraqi tanks), into killing zones.

What happened next is uncertain. Some reports assume that Iranian regulars recognized the nature of this operation as a 'diversion', and did not press home their attack, prompting reports about 'half-hearted' efforts.[88] Yet it was the IRIA which cracked open the Iraqi defences in several places. The IRGC, which lacked armour, failed to reinforce spearheads on time. Isolated, these had to fight their way back to their start-line. Another attack hit the Iraqi 16th Infantry Division during the night of 17 – 18 January, but any gains were quickly lost to counter-attacks. A day later, the Iranians called off their operation; while claiming to have taken up to 260 square kilometres of Iraqi territory, they failed to take Naft Shahr or to divert any enemy troops from the south.

This time, it was the Pasdaran who were made scapegoats. An observer from 77th Infantry Division IRIA commented that while the final approach was supposed to be made silently, the Basiji opened fire, forcing army's commanders to launch their assault before schedule.

Karbala-8

On 9 April 1987, the Iranians launched their next offensive on the Central Front, Operation Karbala-8. This time, it was the IRGC that intended to improve IranianKurdish positions and to divert Iraqi resources northwards. Once again this was a short operation, involving only two divisions. Unsurprisingly, it was broken off within two days, despite taking three heights near Suleimaniya. Rather tragically, it prompted the Iraqis into launching chemical weapon attacks on 20 Kurdish villages, on 15 April 1987.[89]

For the rest of the year, central frontlines remained largely quiet, other than minor clashes. These included Operations like Karbala-9, launched against II Corps in the Qasr-e Shirin area to capture a useful height; Nasr-2, which – supported by 30 IRIAA helicopters and some air strikes of the IRIAF – hit 22nd Infantry Division to gain some ground in the Meimak Heights; Nasr-3, which struck 29th Infantry Division in June; and Nasr-6, which hit 22nd Division between Sumar and the Meimak Heights, in August 1987. Furthermore, during the night of 19 – 20 December 1987, two Pasdaran brigades – reinforced by some commandos – assaulted positions of 29th Division along the Doveyrich River, apparently with some minor success.[90]

CHAPTER 4
THE NORTHERN FRONT 1982-1987

Baghdad's decision to abandon most of its conquests inside Iran left I Corps on the defensive during the period 1982-1987, with a conventional role shielding Sulaymaniyah and a counter-insurgency role containing the Kurds. The year following the Iraqi withdrawal of 1982 was relatively quiet on the northern front until signs of an imminent Iranian offensive led to a pre-emptive operation by the newly-established 24th Infantry Division. This began during the night of 26 – 27 July 1983, east of Qala Diza, and resulted in seizure of two 2,300-metre high peaks in the Jabal Balgha range. While this success came at a heavy cost – because 28th Infantry Division IRIA was alerted on time – the Iranians failed to regain the peaks.

However, between July 1983 and early 1988, the primary battlefields of the northern front were the Haj Umran Pass and the Sulaymaniyah-Penjwin-Marivan roads (where Chwarta became the virtual 'eye of the storm'). These were tantalizingly close to the PUK's eastern sanctuaries of Basilan and Jafati Valley. The events in the two sectors between 1983 and 1987 will be described geographically rather than chronologically to ease understanding.

Haj Umran Sector, 1983-1987

The Haj Umran Pass carries the main road from northwest Iran through Piran Shah, then along mountain ranges at an elevation above 2,000 metres, to Arbil and then Kirkuk. From Kirkuk the road continues southwards in the general direction of Baghdad, but it also meets the highway eastwards to Sulaymaniyah. The pass itself runs between two border massifs with Haj Umran (also Haj Omran) at its mouth. To the north is the 3,874 metre high Shuman

Many of the combatants deployed during the Iranian offensives on the northern sector of the frontlines in 1984 were either Basiji, mobilised form the local population, or KDP Kurds. Here a group of them is preparing for action after being brought to their starting position by one of omni-present Toyota 4WD pickups. (IRGC)

Mustafa (Chumanmostafa) and the River Bala (Balak), which wends down the eastern side of the spur, then westwards to join the River Rawana (Rawand or Rubar). To the south is a massif up to 3,587 metres high, with outcrops dominating the road which then goes up the Rubar-i-Ruwandiz valley, to the town of Rawandiz.[91]

Still led by Dr Abdul Rahman Ghassemlou, the KDPI remained a major thorn in Tehran's side, although driven back towards the border with Iraq. Having forced the KDPI out and into camps in the Rawandiz Valley, just inside Iraq, in 1983 the Iranians prepared a

To accelerate advance of the IRGC forces in the Haj Umran sector of July 1983, the IRIAA made extensive use of its helicopters to deploy light infantry on dominating peaks. (via N. S.)

A PC-7 light strike aircraft seen while overflying forward Iranian positions during Operation Val Fajr-2. (Farzin Nadimi Collection)

'final settling of accounts' with Ghassemlou.

The pre-war garrison of Piran Shahr had been part of the 64th Infantry Division IRIA, most of which was committed to COIN operations, leaving only its 132nd Infantry Battalion behind. Consequently, substantial reinforcements were needed for the offensive – code-named Val Fajr-2. These included 2nd Brigade of 77th Infantry Division, 105th Mechanized Battalion of 92nd Armoured Division IRIA, and a brigade of 33rd al-Mahdi Division IRGC on the northern side. To the south of Piran Shahr were a brigade of 8th Najaf Ashraf Infantry Division, 14th Imam Hossein Infantry Division and a part of 105th Qods Infantry Brigade – all IRGC. This gave the Iranians about 45,000 troops, including the Barzani-led KDP of about 800, and some 200 Iraqi Shi'a 'Mujahideen'. The Kurds not only acted as infantry, but also as scouts and porters of supplies, while the artillery of 64th and 77th Division was bolstered by that of 33rd Artillery Group (battalion each of 130mm howitzers and MRLs). Furthermore, the IRIAA deployed about 30 helicopters from the 4th CSG in support (these evacuated 260 injured soldiers and 39 civilians during this operation, while delivering 40 tonnes of supplies).

The KDP Kurds discovered that the pass was defended only by 23rd Infantry Division's 91st Infantry Brigade, supported by 4th Border Guards Brigade, and the PUK. However, Iraqi spies in Iran alerted the commander of I Corps, Major-General Niima Faris al-Mihyawi. The only uncertainty was when, and where, the main blow would fall.

The attack came during the night of 21 – 22 July, with the Iranians crossing the border in combined formations of IRIA, IRGC and KDP on multiple points along a 30 kilometre wide frontline – primarily through infiltration – to envelop the valley. The main blow came from the south with the rapid seizure of many peaks which the defenders had been unable to garrison.

The push down the road, into the mouth of the valley, faced fierce resistance. This came not only from the KDPI, but from Iraqi helicopter gunships, and – reportedly – mustard gas shells fired by artillery. Whether or not the latter were really deployed, it had little effect because of terrain and weather. Iranian helicopters proved far more effective than those of the Iraqis, who even used two Ilyushin Il-76 transports to bomb Iranian positions, dropping their bombs from the rear loading ramp, though with little effect.[92] Iraqi counter-attacks also proved unsuccessful, and by 26 July the Iranians had advanced 10 kilometres, taking not only Haj Umran, but also 43 villages and Height 2435 (or Kerde Ku). In the south, the Pasdaran

even overcame stiff Kurdish resistance to take Mount Kerde Mand (Kerdemand), and its western heights, which overlooked the town of Rayat, west of Haj Umran.

Two days later, on 28 July 1983, the Iraqis launched their first heliborne assault on Mount Kerde Mand. Supported by air strikes (including some by PC-7s) and artillery, and a mechanised force which isolated the peak, Mi-8s lifted two battalions from 66th Special Forces Brigade, and the Special Forces battalion of the Guards Corps. The initial landing was unopposed, but once on the ground the troops faced fierce resistance and it took them until the next morning to secure the mountain. As soon as the area was secure, special forces troops were relieved by a brigade of 23rd Infantry Division – which lost the peak shortly afterwards, in early August 1983, to an Iranian counterattack. Eventually the fighting fizzled out, leaving the Iranians and their KDP allies holding the key heights dominating the eastern Haj Umran road, while the Iraqis held the heights in the lower valley. Some idea of the scale of the fighting may be gained by the fact that 77th Infantry Division IRIA expended 22 tonnes of 105mm field artillery ammunition and 1,435 mortar bombs in a single day.

Iranian Success

For the Iranians, Val Fajr-2 was a rare successful offensive. The IRIA, the IRGC and the KDP not only recovered 195 square kilometres of Iranian territory but also captured 220 square kilometres of Iraq. They had also cut the main KDPI supply line and forced their survivors to flee westwards, often leaving behind their families, most of whom – up to 20,000 – were held in detention camps in southern Iran. The Iranians gave Barzani's KDP control over the Haj Umran camp area, and they brought in their families from Khaneh, while that town itself was given to the Iraqi Shi'a dissident Dawa Party and Hojatolislam Mohammed Bakr Hakim of the Supreme Council of the Islamic Revolution for Iraq (SCIRI), which was created in 1982.

The Iranian successes in Kurdish territory prompted ever more Kurds to defect from the Iraqi Army and, in August 1983, Baghdad admitted that up to 48,000 Kurdish fighters were absent without leave and might have joined the anti-government insurgency. Nevertheless, the effects of Val Fajr-2 were limited and the Iraqis understood this operation was designed to stretch the Iraqi Army while a larger one, Val Fajr-4, was launched in the south. Yet he Iraqis were always worried that the northern dams might be captured or destroyed, leading to severe flooding in central and even southern Iraq.

Youthful gunners of an Iraqi artillery unit in 1985. (via Ali Tobchi)

Operation Qader

While 1984 remained quiet on the northern front, in 1985 the Iranians belatedly decided to exploit the success of Val Fajr-2 with Operation Qader (Almighty God). This was to be launched northwards from Haj Umran towards Heights 2624, 3874 and 3075 using 77th Infantry Division's 1st Brigade in combination with elements from 23rd, 28th and 64th Divisions and 55th Airborne Brigade IRIA. The IRGC provided a brigade from 8th Najaf Ashraf Division together with the 105th Qods and 155th Seyed ol-Shohada Brigades, which were to advance from Kerde Mand towards the high ground opposite Shuman Mustafa to tighten control of the Haj Umran Pass.

The Iranians struck at dawn on 15 July 1985 and initially they had little success against 431st, 433rd, and 438th Infantry Brigades of 23rd Division. Saddam was concerned enough to send a delegation from the GHQ, including Khairallah and the Operations Chief, Lieutenant-General Hisham Sabah al-Fakhri. Soothing messages were sent south, but on 16 July the Iranians renewed their attack, driving back the defenders until they reached the lower slopes of Heights 2624, 2873, and 3874. Now even the Sidakan Valley was under threat, and GHQ had to despatch reinforcements in the form of commando brigades and artillery units from III, IV, and VI Corps for a counter-attack launched by Brigadier-General Iyad Khalil Zaki al-Bayati's 33rd Infantry Division. Attacks by 428th Infantry Brigade, on 25 July, and by IV Corps' 2nd Commando Brigade, three days later, retook high ground south of the road. Yet during the night of 28 – 29 July, the Iranians struck at 703rd Infantry Brigade, who held the attack when reinforced by VI Corps commandos.

After a three-day break the Iraqis launched counterattacks. During the night of 1 – 2 September 1985, the III Corps' commando brigade attacked in the 33rd Division sector and on the night of 6 – 7 September, 66th Special Forces Brigade secured Height 2030.

Despite this setback, on 9 September the Iranians renewed Qader, striking positions of 23rd and 33rd Divisions on a 50-kilometre front. Armoured forces, with elements of 55th Airborne IRIA Brigade, pushed from Rayat, while infantry advanced towards Sidakan to outflank the enemy. Already on alert – partially with help of intelligence provided by Kurds – the Iraqis held this attack. After the front quietened down, the 66th Special Forces Brigade regained a number of peaks – including Height 2435 – in a combined operation with the PUK during the night of 17 – 18 September, the front then quietened down again.

Karbala-2

While the rest of 1985 remained quiet in the north, during the second half of April 1986, V Corps began raiding Iranian and Kurdish positions near the border. The success of these attacks encouraged a larger operation by 33rd Infantry Division during the night of 10 – 11 May 1985. This took ground above 2,000 metres,

encouraging plans for a major assault upon Kerde Mand. This began during the night of 13 – 14 May in constant rain and regained not only Kerde Mand, but also Kerde Ku, and then drove off all Iranian counterattacks.

During the summer of 1986, the IrAF staged a strategic air campaign against towns behind the frontline. With the IRIAF unable to respond, the SDC decided to retaliate on the ground by taking the entire Haj Umran Valley. Saddam, concerned about another 'Val Fajr 8' publicly appealed to Iran – in August – not to implement its threat to launch a final offensive, and on 3 August produced a FourPoint Peace Plan, but the Iranian response was to launch Operation 'Karbala 2.'

On 1 September, two division-sized task forces; the northern with three brigades from 9th Badr, 10th Seyed o-Shohada, and 155th Divisions IRGC, and the southern with three brigades from 12th Qa'em-e Mohammad, 21st Imam Reza and 105th Qods Divisions, came down the heights and into the valley on either side of the road to Piran Shahr. Due to poor Iranian coordination, and good Iraqi aerial support, the defenders – including 98th, 604th and 807th Infantry Brigades of 33rd Infantry Division in the north, and 91st Infantry Brigade in the south – experienced no problem stopping each attack and within two days Karbala-2 was abandoned with Kerde Man still in Iraqi hands.

Karbala-7

After a lull due to winter, the Iranians decided to support 'Karbala 6' on the Central Front with a diversion which would push further down the Haj Umran Pass. Karbala 7 was launched during the night of 3 to 4 March 1987 by 64th IRIA Infantry Division supported by KDP Kurds. The Iraqi 91st Infantry Brigade fought well and initially contained the assault, but then the Iranians broke through and secured not only Kerde Mand, but advanced for 1-2 kilometres in the direction of Shuman Mustafa. This time, the counterattacks by units of V Corps failed to recover the lost ground, highlighting problems caused by the spread of the Kurdish insurgency, and laid the foundation of the Anfal campaigns (see Chapter 6). Lacking troops to bolster their success, the Iranians were forced to limit their activity to a few raids for the remainder of 1987. The biggest of these was Operation Nasr-7, launched on 5 August by four IRGC brigades which struck 24th Infantry Division's positions around Qala Diza, inside Iran, and drove the Iraqis back across the border. A similar attack upon 23rd Infantry Division – Operation Nasr-9, launched on 23 November 1987 – was less successful.

Chwarta Sector, 1983-1987

The Chwarta Sector is entered through the Mishiyaw Salient, a valley beneath peaks of up to 2,000 metres. Running on an east-west axis through the salient is the Chami-Qizilja (Aw-e Rashia) River, which flows into the Nahr Siwayl. The latter runs past several heights, ranging from 1605-2086 metres, to join the Lower Zab River (al-Zab Saqir) inside a valley north-east of the town known as Chwarta (Churwartah or Chuartah). The latter is about 25 kilometres from Sulaymaniyah and a tantalising 50 kilometres from the Iranian border. The terrain is rugged and there are only a few good roads, indeed even today most 'roads' in this region are mere dirt tracks. The one connecting Chwarta with Sulaymaniyah continues eastwards, passing through the village of Mawat, before crossing the border to join the Iranian frontier road linking Sar Dasht and Baneh. Another road runs northwest from Marivan, across the border to Penjwin, through the valley of the Gogasur before turning south into the intensively cultivated valley north

Youthful Basiji taking a short break prior to continuing their advance towards the next peak during Val Fajr-4. (Albert Grandolini Collection)

Cheerful IRGC troops atop an Iraqi T-55 MBT captured during the Operation Val Fajr-4. (Albert Grandolini Collection)

of Lake Dharband-I Khan. Thirty five kilometres southwest of Penjwein is Halabja.[93]

Val Fajr-4

The Chwarta Sector had been relatively quiet for nearly two years, before the Pasdaran – supported by the KDP – decided to launch an impromptu attack on the northern face of the salient on 16 September 1983. During the following three days they took a number of key heights that proved as useful jumping-off points. To complete the neutralization of the KDPI, the Iranians planned their first major offensive in this sector, Operation Val Fajr-4. This involved the envelopment of the Mishiyaw Salient using Task Force Hamzeh with 30,000 men divided into four battlegroups:

- Hamzeh-1 (two brigades of 14th Imam Hossein IRGC Division and 2nd Brigade from 21st IRIA Infantry Division), and
- Hamzeh-2 (3rd Brigade from 28th IRIA Infantry Division, a tank battalion from 88th IRIA Armoured Division, and part of 44th Qamar Bani Hashem IRGC Engineer Brigade) were to deliver the major blow from the north;
- Hamzeh-3 (two brigades from 8th Najaf Ashraf IRGC Infantry

Division, 2nd Brigade from 28th IRIA Infantry Division).
- Hamzeh-4 (1st Brigade from 28th IRIA Infantry Division) with KDP.

Hamzeh-1 and Hamzeh-2 were to deliver the major blow from the north while the other two battlegroups would strike from the south. Fire support was provided by 11th Artillery Group IRIA (27 batteries with 105mm and 203mm guns, and three MRLS batteries), the 3rd and 4th Combat Support groups IRIAA (total of 42 helicopters).

The Iranian objective was to slice off the salient and take the heights overlooking Marivan in the west, thus preventing the Iraqis from shelling Baneh and Marivan. The secondary objective was to clear the valleys of the KDPI and further disrupt its last major supply-line into Iraq.

Meanwhile the I Corps, commanded by Major-General Maher Abd al-Rashid, was badly over-streched. The sector was held by 4th Infantry Division, which was then re-inforced by 7th Infantry Division – commanded by Brigadier-General Sultan Hashim Ahmed – from II Corps. The salient was now defended six brigades and some Border Guards.

The Iranians opened their attack during the night of 19 – 20 October by infiltrating and then overrunning forward Iraqi positions. Much of 5th Infantry Brigade collapsed, opening the way for the Pasdaran to take Mishiyaw Salient, five KDPI camps, and heights including 1614, 1768 and 2086. A night later, the Iranians put even more pressure upon the defenders, and during the night of 23 – 24 August, they widened the frontline by assaulting most of 4th Infantry Division. Although degenerating into hand-to-hand fighting, their attempt to completely isolate 5th Infantry Brigade failed in the face of a counter-attack which re-took Height 1904 and Kani Manga, northeast of Penjwin. During the battle Iraqi helicopters deployed part of 65th Special Forces Brigade behind enemy lines to interdict communications, while Iraqi airmen flew 122 air, and 39 helicopter sorties, some at night. Although causing heavy casualties, this effort was in vain and the Iraqis evacuated Penjwin on 29 October 1983, although their artillery prevented the enemy from occupying the town.

During the night of 2 – 3 November 1983, Hamzeh-2 struck 7th Infantry Division, forcing it away from Height 1900, but the main Iraqi defence line held firm. This allowed Saddam to send the Guards' Special Forces Brigade to retake Height 1900 during the night of 4 – 5 November.

In the south, the Iranians vainly attempted to occupy Penjwin, on 6 November 1983, but the town remained in no-man's land. Three nights later, two divisions of the IRIA and seven of the IRGC struck both 4th and 7th Infantry Divisions, but failed again. Emboldened, corps commander Maher Abd al-Rashid and his divisional commanders then publically informed Saddam that, '…they had succeeded in a model defence campaign to cause the Iranians a major defeat, and decimated their forces.'[94]

Yet the Iranians had not only captured the Qizilja and Gogasur Valleys, but also some 650 square kilometres of Iraqi territory, pushing the defenders to within 10 kilometres east of Chwarta. Furthermore, Val Fajr-4 had certainly attracted substantial Iraqi strength, and when it concluded each of two Iraqi divisions controlled up to 10 brigades (including four special forces units), making their command at least challenging, if not difficult. Furthermore, in the wake of Val Fajr-2 in the north it helped encourage the growth of the Kurdish rebellion in northern Iraq.

Val Fajr-9

Val Fajr-4 left the Iranians only 40 kilometres from Sulaymaniya and poised to reach at least the Lower Zab Valley. For the SDC this was an excellent opportunity to 'spook' the Iraqis and divert them as Iran launched its offensive on the Faw Peninsula, Val Fajr-8. Nevertheless, the Iraqis realized this was a diversion thanks to their Kurdish scouts and COMINT.

Spearheaded by the 57th Albolfazl al-Abbas Infantry Brigade – supported by 105th Qods, 110th Boroujerdi, and 155th Brigade IRGC, and a brigade of 28th Infantry Division – the Iranians attacked into the Katu range around Heights 1543 and 1451 during the night of 24 – 25 February. The thin Iraqi line was soon overwhelmed, but the 34th Infantry Division managed to hold most of its major positions, while commandos and Kurdish NDBs launched counterattacks to recover peaks overlooking the Zab Valley.

Further south, 27th Infantry Division found itself exposed to another attack, but successfully held its lines, encouraging its commanders to launch a counter-attack and regain terrain ranging from 1,800-2,100 metres – especially all the peaks lost during the October-November 1983 campaign.

The 34th Division counter-attacked during the night of 5 – 6 March 1986, through cloud and continuous rain (which turned to snow on the higher ground), with helicopter and artillery support. While it was not completely successful, it did regain many of the heights and cleared the area up to the border by 14 March. Reinforced by the Guards' Special Forces Brigade and NDBs, 27th Infantry Division counter-attacked during the night of 20 – 21 March and retook additional heights. Finally, both divisions launched another attack during the night of 27 – 28 March and recovered most of the lost ground. Nevertheless, the Iranians were barely five kilometres

Some of the Iraqi POWs captured during Karbala-10. (Albert Grandolini Collection)

Iranian Army troops and the Pasdaran made extensive use of RPG-7s for attacks on Iraqi fortifications during the Operations Val Fajr-9 and Karbala-10. (Tom Cooper Collection)

from Chwarta, and had extended their hold down the western slopes of the last heights before Sulaymaniyah, which lay only 15 kilometres away.

Karbala-10

Determined to maintain pressure, the Iranians prepared their next offensive – Karbala-10 – aiming to take Mawat, some 30 kilometres to the northwest to provide better communications for the pro-Barzani Kurds. The attack would be launched by Task Force Ramadan (110th Boroujerdi Infantry Brigade and 9th Badr Infantry Division, totalling about 12,000 troops), and KDP forces, which faced V Corps' 34th and 39th Infantry Divisions. Karbala-10 also envisaged two sub-operations: Nasr-1, run by Task Force Ramadan, and a combined PUK/Iranian commando – Operation Fath-5.

The Iraqis had been aware of the impeding blow since 20 April, but lacked details. Consequently, when the Pasdaran assaulted three nights later, they quickly captured some 20 villages and heights east of the Lower Zab, 1972 and 1897, which dominating the confluence of the rivers. Despite the IRGC concentrating a total of 77 infantry battalions, Karbala-10 was contained in early June 1987 with the help of reinforcements rushed from Baghdad.

Nasr-4, -5, -7, -8 and -9

Dissatisfied with results of Karbala-10, the SDC transferred the sector to the headquarters of Task Force Najaf, while Brigadier-General Ali Siyed Shirazi personally planned the next offensive – Operation Nasr-4. Launched during the night of 20 – 21 June 1987, this attack took the remaining heights around Mawat and the village

of Zhazaya, pushing 39th Infantry Division back across the Lower Zab. Three nights later, Task Force Najaf launched Operation Nasr-5, this time driving back the southern flank of 34th Infantry Division.

Saddam reacted by rushing reinforcements – including the Guards Baghdad Infantry Division, and 3rd and 16th Special Forces Brigades. These helped 34th and 39th Divisions to counter-attack during the night to 26 June and regain some heights but left the Iranians overlooking Mawat and the nearby Lower Zab Valley.

Rafsanjani claimed these successes were 'as important as those at Faw Peninsula, because… Suleymaniyah is an entrance gate to other parts of Iraq', but while the Iranians were now closer to Sulamaniyeh, and only 100 kilometres from Kirkuk and its oil fields, they could not exploit their successes. Task Force Najaf also launched its third operation, Nasr-7, from the night of 4 – 5 August 1987 using parts of 7th Vali Asr and 27th Mohammad Rasoolallah IRGC Infantry Divisions, which managed to push 24th and 39th Infantry Divisions from additional heights.

There were two additional Iranian 'land grabs'; Operations Nasr-8 and -9 at the end of 1987. During the night of 20 – 21 November, brigades from 11th Amir al-Momenin, 12th Qa'em-e Mohammad, 21st Imam Reza, 57th Abolfazl al-Abbas, and 155th Seyed ol-Shohada IRGC Infantry Divisions attacked the new 44th in Mawat sector and pushed it back, taking Height 1107 (called Mount Girdarash by the Iranians) in the process. By contrast, Nasr-9 was a vain enterprise launched during the night of 21 – 22 September by 2nd Brigade 64th IRIA Infantry Division.

CHAPTER 5
IRAN'S LAST CHANCE

Following the bloody failures around Basra (see Volume 3), and with the passing of Khomeini's deadline for 'final victory' by 31 March 1987, the SDC reconsidered its strategic options. Finally concluding that taking Basra was extremely unlikely, it decided to switch the strategic focus northwards, and press deeper into northern Iraq with Kurdish support. A key factor for this decision was the existence of extensive areas – 'sanctuaries' – held by the PUK around Suleymaniyah. Calculating that by opening routes to these, Iran could secure a massive enclave inside Iraq to threaten not only Suleymaniyah but also the northern oil fields, the SDC decided to switch its prime strategic objectives from the Southern to the Northern Front. Consequently, nearly a dozen IRGC divisions began making their way from southern to northern Iran. Due to the nature of the ramshackle communications system, it took them months to complete this journey and they did not assemble until late 1987. When they arrived many divisions were broken up, often with one brigade being deployed in a separate sector possibly to 'stiffen' their IRIA garrisons. Their arrival was an omen of a radical change in the Iranian strategy in this war, because the northern front had largely been a backwater for conventional operations during the past seven years.

Beit-ol-Mogaddas-2, -3 and -6

The first attempt to reach the 'sanctuaries' was Operation Beit-ol-Moghaddas 2, launched from the Chwarta area on 15 January

Troops of one of the IRGC's naval brigades marching into the hills in the Chwrata area, in January 1988. (via N. S.)

1988, with the aim of reaching the PUK-controlled Jafati Valley. Five brigades struck southwest from Height 1107, driving 39th and 44th Infantry Divisions back towards the Lower Zab Valley by 21 January. Further tightening their grip on Mawat, the Iranians then established a bridgehead across the Zab (between Heights 1707 and 1827) adding another 130 square kilometres of Iraqi territory.

Two months later, on 15 March 1988, brigades form 5th Nasr and 31st Ashura IRGC Infantry Divisions on the right, and 12th Qaem-e-Mohammad IRGC Infantry Division (reinforced with

The task of resupplying infantry brigades cut off by Iranian offensives of early 1988 proved a very dangerous one; a number of IrAAC Mi-8/17 helicopters were shot down by the Iranians, while hauling 'beans, bullets and gas' for Iraqi ground troops. (IRIA)

Bad weather concealed much of the Iranian troop movements on the northern frontlines in the period January-May 1988. (via N. S.)

35th Imam Hassan and 48th Fath al-Mustaqil Brigades) on the left, stormed the southern heights and occupied the area southwest of Mawat, around Height 1827.[95]

With the road to the sanctuary still blocked, Beit-ol-Moghaddas-6 was launched from 16 to 18 May, using brigades from three divisions, which took Height 1827 from 44th Division. However, once there, the Iranians could not advance any further. Even so, their total gains included another 25 square kilometres of sparsely populated territory and 750 prisoners.[96]

Chief-of-Staff Khazraji was not pleased about the performance of the 38th Infantry Division in the Lake Dukan area, and made his views clear when he evaluated the defence at a conference with Saddam. He described the performance of 448th Infantry Brigade as 'terrible' and noted 76th and 442nd Infantry Brigades were isolated and had to be resupplied by helicopters, and while although increasing the number of brigades deployed in the Qalat Dizah sector from three to seven, Khazraji demanded additional reinforcements. [97]

The Iranian success prompted an adverse reaction from Turkey. Ankara was then controlled by secular Sunnis, who were always suspicious of Iran's theocratic Shi'a regime – and even more so to the Iranian success in northern Iraq. Turkey therefore threatened to close the border and – following an air attack on 27 March 1988 – reinforced its garrisons in the adjacent area.

Lake Darband-i-Khan

While the Iranian government might be concerned about the closure of the border, the I SDC was more interested in the sector to the south, around the town of Halabja (also Halabcheh), a town of some 70,000 people, mostly Kurds. This sector was separated from Iran by the 1,500-3,000 metre high Shamran range, which stretches for 60 kilometres from Penjwin to the River Sirvan. Halabja is in the centre of a fertile belt arcing around the Daraband-i-Khan Lake, only some 20 kilometres from the border – as the crow flies. The lake held three billion cubic metres of water, but was subject to frequent slope failure requiring constant repair. On its southern end a 128-metre high, 445 metre long, US-designed dam was constructed in 1961. This generated nearly 40 per cent of Iraqi's electricity. German and Japanese companies launched the work on replacing its two original 800kW generators with two 83MW units in 1983, but this work was completely only in 1990.[98]

Shielding the approaches to the southern part of the lake from Iran are a series of 1,600-2,900 metre heights, of which the most important are 2945 (Sindravi) and 1802 (Shakh-e Balambo). Across the river are Heights 1108 (Shakh-e-surmer) and 1306 (Shakh-e-shemiran). In March the temperature in the region averages 17C but can drop to 5.5C; during the summer, it rises rapidly to 39.5°C. Given the predominance of Kurds in the region, this front had naturally attracted insurgent presence; indeed, these were covertly present in the town for nearly 30 years. In May 1987, this prompted the Iraqi authorities to bulldoze two of the town's quarters, although the population had meanwhile swelled by 60,000 refugees.

Since Operation Tahrir al-Qods in February 1984, the Iranians had launched several attempts to support the Kurds in Halabja. Most of these resulted in minor gains, while Operation Val Fajr-9 (see Chwarta section) ended with an Iraqi defensive success.[99] Realising the Halabja sector was relatively lightly protected, the Iranian commanders believed they could link-up with the PUK-controlled sanctuary in the Qara Dagh Heights. The resulting plan – code-named Operation Val Fajr-10 – envisaged deployment of no less than nine infantry divisions of the IRGC, one of the IRIA, and eleven brigades, for a total of 130,000 troops (see Table 6). In the north, Task Force Qods was to sweep down through the fertile area and cut the road between Sayyid Sadiq and Khurmal. In the south, Task Force Samene-al-Aeme would strike westwards to take Heights 2322 and 2945 then sweep down their slopes to take Halabja. Meanwhile, Task Force Fath would complete Halabja's isolation from the south. Following intensive preparations, the IRIAF was to provide eight F-4E Phantoms from TFB.3 and additional F-5Es from TFB.4 for support of this operation. The IRIAF readied no fewer than 49 helicopters – including 16 AH-1s. The Iraqis were forewarned about the coming attack – in part by increasing activity of the Iranian artillery – but did little to reinforce its three divisions deployed in this area.

Table 6: Order of Battle for Operation Val Fajr-10, April 1988

Corps	Division	Brigades
Iran		
Task Force Qods	41st Sarallah Infantry Division IRGC	
	105th Qods Infantry Division IRGC	
	39th Nabi al-Akram Infantry Brigade IRGC	
	44th Qamar Bani Hashem Engineer Brigade IRGC	
	48th Malek-e Ashtar Infantry Brigade IRGC	
Task Force Samene-ol-Aeme	25th Karbala Infantry Division IRGC	
	27th Mohammad Rasoolallah Infantry Division IRGC	
	31st Ashura Infantry Division IRGC	
	15th Imam Hassan Infantry Brigade IRGC	
	100th Ansal ar-Rasool Infantry Brigade IRGC	
	125th Abu Zayr Infantry Brigade IRGC	
	129th Mayssam Infantry Brigade IRGC	
	142nd Infantry Brigade IRGC	
	77th Nabbovat Commando Brigade IRGC	
	87th Ressalat Artillery Brigade IRGC	
	40th Saheb az-Zaman Engineer Division IRGC	
	84th Infantry Division IRIA	
	55th Airborne Division IRIA	1 brigade
Task Force Fath	9th Badr Infantry Division IRGC	
	10th Seyed o-Shohada Infantry Division IRGC	
	32nd al-Husayn Infantry Division IRGC	
	33rd al-Mahdi Infantry Division IRGC	
	18th al-Ghadir Infantry Brigade IRGC	
	57th Abolfazl al-Abbas Infantry Brigade IRGC	
	49th Muslim Ibn Aqil Infantry Brigade IRGC	
	127th Meghdad Infantry Brigade IRGC	
	11th & 44th Artillery Groups IRIA	
	1st and 2nd CSG, 4th GSG IRIAA	
Iraq		
I Corps	Corps troops, 65th, 66th, 68th Special Forces Brigades, I Corps Artillery Brigade	
	27th Infantry Division	72nd, 119th, 806th Infantry Brigades
	36th Infantry Division	106th, 238th, 426th, 602nd Infantry Brigades
	43rd Division Task Force	87th, 423rd Infantry Brigades
Reinforcements	10th Armoured Division	17th, 42nd, 70th & 80th Armoured Brigades; 24th & 46th Mechanised Brigades
	28th Infantry Division	78th, 412th, 417th Infantry Brigades
	34th Infantry Division	72nd, 76th, 424th, 504th Infantry Brigades
	40th Infantry Division	82nd & 98th Infantry Brigades
	1st Wing IrAAC	

Val Fajr-10

The Iranian assault began during the night of 13 – 14 March 1988, with raids by Iranian commandos (Operation Zafar-7) from the Qara Dagh sanctuary towards Khurmal, with the aim of opening a route towards the Iranian border. Task Forces Qods and Samene-al-Aeme then assaulted positions of 27th and 43rd Divisions, while Fath attacked 36th Infantry Division, positioned on the boundary between I and II Corps.[100] The Iranians overran or outflanked the mountain strong points, with many defenders fleeing westwards, as 'Qods' brushed aside the 43rd Division's mountain defences and swept down to take Khurmal. Its success exposed the defences on Height 1322, and so the Iraqis' line of mountain bastions fell like a row of dominoes. The Iranian advance was aided by air support with the IRIAF flying the first of 99 sorties from the morning of 15 March, with its F-4Es using domestically-produced Shahin-2 air-to-ground rockets for the first time. The Cobra gunships of the IRIAAC flew 588 sorties while helicopters moved forward 5,778 troops and 177 tonnes of supplies, and evacuated 4,808 wounded and civilians during the offensive.

Under this onslaught, the Iraqi 43rd Infantry Division fell apart. It not only suffered over 4,000 casualties, but also had its headquarters overrun and its commander captured – together with up to 1,700 of his troops and about 200 armoured fighting vehicles. Consequently, by 16 March the Pasdaran and PUK were entering Halabja. Meanwhile, Task force Fath took Zimkan and then stormed Height 1802.[101]

Facing less pressure, 27th Infantry Division managed to hold most of its frontline, but had to swing back its right flank to keep the Iranians outside Sayyid Saddiq, pending the arrival of reinforcements from II Corps – including 28th Infantry Division, 70th and 80th Armoured Brigades (17th Armoured Division), and 46th Mechanised Brigade (12th Armoured Division). The IrAF and the IrAAC fought back as intensively as they could; fighter-bombers flew 104 sorties on 19 March 1988 alone, while helicopters are known to have flown 613 sorties between 16 and 19 March.

When all of this showed little effect, Saddam ordered the IrAF to deploy chemical weapons against major Iranian concentrations in and around Halabja. These were launched starting on the morning

A post-Iran-Iraq War photograph of Lake Daraband-i-Khan. (Mark Lepko Collection)

A column of the Pasdaran on a march in Halabja area in March 1988. (Farzin Nadimi Collection)

The Iranian Army deployed two of its Artillery Groups (the 11th and the 44th) in support of Operation Val Fajr-10. This photograph shows a M109 155mm self-propelled howitzer on the march towards the front. (via N. S.)

Troops of one of the IRGC's naval brigades seen in positions recently captured from the Iraqis, during the Operaiton Val Fajr-10. (Farzin Nadimi Collection)

Pasdaran bringing their wounded back to starting positions. (Farzin Nadimi Collection)

of 16 March 1988, and included more than 50 MiG-21s, Mirage F.1EQs, PC-7s and Su-22s. The brunt of the bombs filled with nerve agents fell upon Halabja. Tragically, very few Iranian troops were in the town, but nearly 4,000 civilians – men, women, and children – perished. The carnage increased when the Iraqi artillery then bombarded the town with a mix of high-explosive and gas-filled shells.[102] Khazraji would later claim that neither he, nor any military leader, was involved in the decision which was taken by Saddam, Majid and military production chief Hussein Kamel; while Saddam denied all knowledge of the decision and blamed Khazraji.

The horror of Halabja overshadowed the rest of the campaign, with the advance slowing by 19 March as the Iranians outran their supplies. Task Force Qods reached towards Sayyid Sadiq, but were held along the Alas-i-yaw, while the Qara Dagh sanctuary was still 35 kilometres away. Meanwhile, Iraqi reinforcements from IV and V Corps poured to fill the gaps in the breached frontline. The exhausted Iranians began to dig in after advancing up to 30 kilometres to the lake's eastern shore down to the Zimkan, and having taken 3,000 prisoners.

The second phase thus began on 27 March 1988, when Task Force Fath launched Operation Beit-ol-Moghaddas-4 against 36th Infantry Division, using T-72 MBTs captured only days previously, but were beaten off. During the night of 9 – 10 April, the Iranians opened Operation Beit-ol-Moghaddas-5 in the Penjwin sector, seized many heights and inflicted heavy losses upon 27th Infantry Division. Further south, Task Force Qods (meanwhile including IRGC's divisions Seyed ol-Shohada and Mohammad Rasoolallah, and brigades al-Ghadir and Abolfazl al-Abbas) infiltrated across the Zimak during the evening of 10 – 11 April, to hit 36th Infantry Division. They reached Heights 1108 and 1306 to extend their grip along the lake's eastern shore for a further five kilometres to the mouth of the Zimkn Valley. However, this attack petered out by 19 April 1988, primarily because of events on the Southern Front (see

Volume 3).[103]

In early April Baghdad was apparently sending all the units it could find as reinforcements, including half the Guards Baghdad Division and 24th and 25th Guards Commando Brigades.[104] On 16 April 1988, Defence Minister Adnan Khairallah made a highly-publicised appearance in Suleymaniyah, but his visit and the 'reinforcements' were designed to divert Iranian attention from the Faw Peninsula where Iraq struck on 17 April.

The shock of this offensive immediately ended Iranian operations around Lake Darband-i Khan, but Iraqi firepower had already thwarted Iranian ambitions. The IrAF was now flying some 224 combat sorties a day, aided by 31 artillery battalions (560 guns), allowing the defenders to rebuild their defences by early April and gradually they began to push back the Iranians, making much use of chemical weapons, to stabilise the Halabja sector. The Iraqis noted that the Pasdaran were increasingly splitting their divisions into assault and follow-up units, a concept first used by the Imperial German Army in 1918.[105]

Saddam's Discussions

Val Fajr-10 prompted a number of conferences in Baghdad, in the course of which Saddam noted the Iranians now had large forces deployed in the north. He credited this to I and V Corps pinning down the enemy, and therefore ordered a number of spoiling operations, aimed to have maximum effect for minimum casualties. Uncertain whether or not to reinforce I Corps, he said: "We have to ask if the enemy's concentration in that area provides us with an opportunity to strike it in a serious way, to confront and crush them?" There were two ways to achieve this aim; either by a decisive battle, or a war of attrition. Eventually, Chief-of-Staff Khazraji, convinced him to continue the planned offensives on the Southern Front, and once they were completed, use the victorious forces to strike on the Central and then Northern Fronts; advice which Saddam heeded.

The situation on the Northern Front was again discussed on 26 June 1988 during talks about strategy. Saddam appeared pessimistic while Khazraji was optimistic, as was the Operations Chief Lieutenant-General Hussein Rashid. The former explained: "We have sufficient forces, with a simple manoeuvre, we can be a real threat to the enemy in his current position."

A sceptical Saddam, who was worried 28th Infantry Division would be isolated, asked: "'Why Halabja?' and added, 'I don't feel comfortable. What does Halabja mean to us?"

Khazraji countered by pointing out the propaganda value, while Khairallah said the front could be secured by adding another two brigades to the eight already deployed. However, the meeting ended without a decision.[106]

Iranian troops inside a trench in the Halabja area. (via S. N.)

A CH-47C Chinook helicopter, of the IRIAA, seen while unloading casualties collected at a forward position during Val Fajr-10 in March 1988. (Tom Cooper Collection)

Only a day later, Saddam presided another meeting of his senior commanders. This time, Khazraji pointed out that the Halabja front had been reinforced to 13 brigades, while Khairallah suggested the use of six of these for recapturing the town. This idea was eventually accepted, with the operation in question being limited to 21 days for immediate objectives, and seven for the further ones.[107]

The Iraqi Riposte

In fact the Iraqi worries were pointless, for the stunning Iraqi victory on the Faw Peninsula of mid-April 1988 ended all major Iranian offensive activity on the Northern Front. Indeed, the deteriorating situation in the south forced the Iranians to begin withdrawing troops to meet the new threats.

This threat would increase with the Central Front's Operation Tawakkalna ala-Allah-3, and to exploit the increasing enemy weakness a new offensive was planned in the North. Operation Mohammad Rasul Allah (Mohammed, the Messenger of God) aimed to regain all the lost territories around Lake Daraband-i-Khan, around Chwarta and the Haj Umran Pas.

The Mawat sector was the first to feel Iraqi revenge when Major General Sultan Hashim Ahmed's I Corps attacked at dawn on 14 June using 4th, 7th and 44th Infantry Divisions, reinforced by commandos. These advanced in divisional columns to strike five mountain ranges. After 16 hours hard fighting, most of the peaks were in Iraqi hands exposing the Iranians in the valleys. The attack continued on 17 June with the divisions storming a dozen peaks

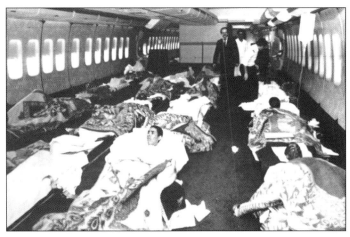

The number of casualties caused by the massive deployment of chemical weapons by the Iraqi military in 1987 and 1988 forced the Iranians to send some of the injured for treatment at specialised facilities abroad. This photograph shows a group of wounded flown to Vienna International on board a Boeing 747 of IranAir. (Albert Grandolini Collection)

A group of Iranian civilian experts and military officers inspecting an unexploded Iraqi bomb. Gauging by its shape, the weapon in question was probably made by the Spanish company Expal, and based on the Mk.82 design of US origin. (Albert Grandolini Collection)

A lot of overhaul and maintenance of their own and captured Iraqi military vehicles in Iran was undertaken in small, privately owned workshops, often under the most rudimentary conditions. (via N. S.)

Wearing a gas mask, this Iranian soldier is demonstrating the effects of Iraqi chemical weapons – in the form of dead birds collected around the battlefield. (Albert Grandolini Collection)

(the 44th Infantry Division distinguished itself by taking Height 1897 which dominated the Mawat valley). Iranian counter-attacks were beaten off with support of armour, artillery and from the air, and the Pasdaran were left with little other choice but to retreat while blowing up bridges and culverts, as well as laying extensive minefields.[108]

The Iraqis now expanded the scope of the operation, using their reinforcements including 10th Armoured Division and 28th Infantry Division. The 39th Infantry Division, reinforced by commandos, special forces and armour, attacked the Mawat valley on the evening of 29 June and began fighting its way to the border where it was joined on 9 July by 46th Infantry Division. On the night of 9 – 10 July the 27th Infantry Division struck in the Penjwin sector and began working its way through the mountains to the border, severely damaging the former Pasdaran armoured division, 30th 'Beit-ol-Moghaddas'. To stiffen the front, brigades of 28th Infantry Division IRIA with a brigade of 25th Karbala Division, and part of 23rd Special Forces Division IRIA, counter-attacked on the night of 12 – 13 July but were driven back. The V Corps' contribution was on the night of 4 – 5 July when 24th Infantry Division, supported by commandos, armour, and artillery attacked between the Haj Umran-Rawandiz road and Lake Dukan, through terrain of up to 2,300 metres height. The well-coordinated attacks ensured that by the end of the day the Iraqis had totally regained the pass, despite a

rear-guard action by a brigade of 64th Infantry Division, a special forces battalion IRIA, two Pasdaran battalions and Gendarmerie in the heights shielding the road to Piran Shahr.

From mid-June 1988, around Lake Darband-i-Khan, the 36th Infantry Division had begun attacks aimed at regaining the heights southeast of the lake; while 34th Infantry Division struck towards Sayyid Sadiq. Strong defences meant that the Iraqis made little progress. Defence Minister Khairallah now returned to the front and sought a renewed attack, for which corps commander Sultan Hashim Ahmed transferred 10th Armoured Division from the north, and reinforced it with four infantry brigades. It was brought in beside 34th Division and launched a surprise attack in the Sayid Sadiq sector on 12 July, overcoming defences. However, it's further advance was eventually stopped by Iranian demolition work on the roads, which were also cut by deep trenches and covered from the heights.

Meanwhile, there was intense diplomatic activity as the United Nations sponsored a cease-fire; to accelerate this as his forces disintegrated, on 15 July Rafsanjani announced the withdrawal of Iranian forces from Iraqi territory, which began the next day. This opened the way for the 34th Division to retake Halabja, and eased the Iraqi advance towards the border. Siriwn was liberated by 15 July, and by 20 July 1988 the Iraqis had reached the border. Simultaneously, 36th Infantry Division retook the border heights to end the conventional war in the north.

CHAPTER 6
THE KURDISH FRONT 1980-1988

The low-intensity operations of the Kurdish Front sprawled across the tri-state border with fighting in eastern Turkey even before the Iran-Iraq War. The Kurds represented around 15 per cent of Turkey's population and their determination to seek autonomy had seen major revolts throughout the life of Kemal Ataturk, founder of modern Turkey, with hundreds of thousands of Kurds displaced and Istanbul banning Kurdish culture. From 1980, Turkey described

the minority as Easterners (Doğulu). In the 1970s the Kurds were split between those who sought autonomy through political action, which had some success, and the Kurdistan Workers Party (Partiya Karkerên Kurdistan) or PKK, which launched 'armed struggle'. The PKK's war against Turkey grew ever more intense through the late 1970s and early 1980s. With the Iranian Revolution in 1979 the Kurdish struggle rolled across the border into north-western Iran,

Kurdish people of northern Iraq. After more than 20 years of almost-constant insurgency against the central government in Baghdad, much of the local society was militarised and most of the young men under arms. (Mark Lepko collection)

Shirazi with KDPI leaders. (IRGC)

as described above.

The Iraqi invasion of 1980 prompted Ghassemlou and his KDPI to reposition their headquarters to the Iraqi village of Sunn, near Halabja. Strengthened by Baghdad's arms and supplies and exploiting Iran's problems with the Iraqi invasion and insurgencies in north-western Iran, in April 1981 he struck towards Lake Urumia, Mahabad, Naqadeh, Bukan and Saqqez with 7,000-12,000 Peshmerga. In Sanandaj, they encircled 64th Infantry Division's 1st Brigade. After a month-long siege, the brigade ran out of ammunition and had to surrender, having lost nearly half the garrison, but killing nearly 2,000 of the attackers.[109] The 64th Infantry Division's 3rd Brigade in Marivan held out and, with his men exhausted and short of supplies, Ghassemlou was forced to withdraw.

Gambling that the KDPI's offensive had run out of steam, Bani-Sadr concentrated his limited military resources against the uprising in the nearby Azerbaijan province instead. However, this handed more ammunition to his critics, and in June 1981 he was dismissed by Khomeini. Immediately afterwards, Tehran concentrated 100,000 troops (including about 30,000 Pasdaran, several thousand Gendarmes, and Barzani's supporters) for an offensive against about 15,000 KDPI Peshmerga. Spearheaded by 16th IRIA Armoured Division, this force struck westwards and took the Ghassmelou by surprise recovering Sanandaj and then lifting the siege of Marivan, before securing the main road network by taking Saqqez, Bukan, Mahabad, Piranshar, Naqadeh and Urumia. A wave of brutal repression over the local population followed, but despite this setback Ghassemlou planned to launch a new offensive in 1982 with intention of establishing a 'Liberated Kurdish Zone'.

The Iranian Army's Chief-of-Staff, General Shirazi, beat him to the punch. In April 1982, he preempted the KDPI offensive by reinforcing Mahabad, and securing Bukan, Saqqez and Sanandaj. Unsurprisingly, the Peshmerga's attempt to take Mahabad on 26 June was defeated. Although Kurdish insurgents subsequently controlled large parts of the countryside, the Iranians controlled at least most of the valleys.

In mid-September 1982 the Iranians renewed their offensive to clear the main road south of Lake Urmia along the border through the Gharbi Mountains, between Piran Shahr and Sar Dasht, as well as Baneh to Saqqez in the KDPI heartland, and through the 25 kilometre-deep enclave from the frontier. Shirazi used 40,000 men of the IRIA's 16th Armoured, 28th and 64th Infantry Divisions, and a similar number of Pasdaran and Gendarmerie, in a series of small but powerfully-supported offensives. Casualties were heavy on both sides – but especially between Iranians. As one of veterans of 28th Division recalled:

The word was the Peshmerga were born with a rifle in their hands. Their aim was fantastic. They were ambushing us all the time. Lots of our soldiers were killed by head-shots.[110]

While some roads were secured, the KDPI held the Sar Desht-Baneh section. Nevertheless, even this meagre success encouraged the SDC to end the Kurdish threat once and for all, and Shirazi was assigned four IRIA and six IRGC divisions, supported by 300 guns, about 100 MBTs, and 50 helicopters for a new offensive.[111] During the second week of March 1983, Iranian Special Forces deployed by helicopters to block routes from Iraq, while the main body swamped dissident territory south of Lake Urumia. Ghassemlou's attempts to simultaneously fight a mobile guerrilla war and static defence proved disastrous, and within days the Peshmerga were short on ammunition and forced to withdraw into the mountains.

The KDPI now controlled only Baneh and the smaller towns of Oshnavieh and Gavileh, which Ghassemlou decided to retain with defensive operations based upon his Iraqi bases and headquarters in the Haj Umran Pass.

But Shirazi gave him no time to regroup and on 22 July followed up with Operation Val Fajr 2 (see above), in the course of which the Peshmerga were driven out of Iran. During the following years, the surviving members of the KDPI were limited to acting as auxiliaries to the Iraqi Army, before an internecine struggle resulted in a disillusioned Ghassemlou seeking safety in exile in Austria, but he was assassinated in Vienna in 1989. As for Husseini, he decided that discretion was the better part of valour and ceased any kind of military activities against Tehran. He went into exile in Sweden, in 1991, and died there 20 years later.

Iraq's Kurdish Kaleidoscope

Recognizing the impotence of the KDPI, Baghdad subsequently re-routed its support to the PUK. However, if Tehran began 1983 believing it had neutralised the Kurdish threat, Saddam Hussein faced a growing threat.

The Kurdish Front in Iraq covered the border provinces of Dahuk, Arbil, Sulaymaniyah and Diyala, and also touched the inland provinces of Niniwa (round Mosul) and at-Tamim (around Kirkuk), although the latter two were predominantly populated by Arabs and Turkomen as of that time. This area is characterised by terrain over 500 metres above sea level, with mountains in the east, and numerous streams and minor rivers. Many of the slopes were wooded, with meadows and stony fields at their base, the exception being the fertile uplands of the Germain (Gamiyan) – or 'Warm Country' – a the fertile high plain around Qadir Karam, southeast of Kirkuk.

In 1980, Iraqi COIN efforts were centred around three divisions (4th Mountain, 8th and 11th Infantry) deployed in Arbil and Dahuk provinces, and two (2nd and 7th Infantry) deployed in Suleimaniyah province, augmented by Border Guards and Police.[112] Saddam did not rely purely upon military force, but adopted a policy of 'divide and rule' which skilfully exploited the fragmentation of Kurdish society. This meant he was able to withdraw many army units urgently needed for the war with Iran.[113] Left to the para-military forces, the security in the Kurdish areas slowly declined.

The decline began in 1980 when the KDP joined the National Democratic and Patriotic Front – an alliance of anti-Saddam organisations including the Communists and the Kurdistan Socialist Party, which also encouraged any action against the PUK. In April 1981, the Front launched an offensive in Arbil Province against its competition, but the PUK hit back very hard and destroyed most of the Communists. Nevertheless, the kaleidoscopic nature of Kurdish relations meant that only 16 months later the KDP and PUK staged a joint operation in Suleymaniyah.[114]

The departure of the Iraqi Army and the reluctance of the paramilitary forces to run serious COIN operations in the mountains deprived the government of the symbols of power; teachers, medical staff, administrators of protection. Self-preservation compelled local people to withdraw to safety in the larger, and better protected, urban conurbations. Into this power vacuum came the Peshmerga who brought their own administrators, teachers, and doctors to extend their influence from the remotest mountain villages down the slopes to ever larger communities to create liberated areas. The weakness of the counter-insurgency forces eased supply problems for the Kurds; they were unable to provide effective control of the 5-30 kilometre deep belt along the border which had been cleared

Two Kurdish militants in northern Iraq in the mid-1980s. Both are wearing a mix of civilian clothes and military fatigues. Their armament consists of a PKM machine gun (left) and a Dragunov sniper rifle. (Albert Grandolini Collection)

The PUK consisted of a mix of older veterans of earlier Kurdish uprisings and many youngsters, mostly armed with variants of the omnipresent AK-47/AKM-family of assault rifles. (Albert Grandolini Collection)

of some 500 villages – the majority in Sulaymaniyah Province – and 200,000 people forcibly resettled in the south with thousands of other Kurdish civilians after the 1974-1975 revolt. Some of these now began to return and were joined by exiles from Turkey and Iran, while Baghdad actually transferred some refugees north to camps around the city of Arbil. The PKK were also attracted into northern Arbil and Dahuk.[115]

The elimination of the KDPI suited the Barzanis, whose Peshmerga began to extend their control of the border in Arbil Province. This process was further boosted by Iraqi setbacks of 1982, when Baghdad's cancellation of cultural concessions sparked protest demonstrations in Iraq's Kurdish cities and increased skirmishing between Kurds and Iraqi security forces. Nevertheless, the primary threat for Iraqi authority as of early 1983 remained Jalal Talabani, who had thousands of men under arms in Suleymaniyah and Arbil.[116]

With the KDPI's fortunes clearly on the wane, Talabani needed a strong ally to shield himself from Iranian vengeance and reluctantly made common cause with Saddam. An agreement was hammered out on 10 December 1983 in which Talabani pledged not to attack Saddam's forces, and vowed to drive the 'Persians' across the border and fight them in their country – provided Baghdad left him alone. Talabani went further and agreed his Peshmerga would act as Kurdish Border Guards, although some 3,000 reportedly defected to the KDP in protest. A formal ceasefire was signed on 3 January 1984, but Saddam sought to convert this into a long term political solution and dangled the carrot of a renewed commitment to Kurdish autonomy, with Talabani as acknowledged Kurdish leader. For the time being, Saddam was willing to accept Talabani's pledges at face value, but he was aware the PUK was sponsored by Saddam's sworn enemy – Syrian President Hafez al-Assad. Correspondingly, the strongman in Baghdad aimed to buy time until he could settle accounts with the Kurds. Unsurprisingly, his Foreign Minister, Tariq Aziz, warned the Kurds: "If you help us, we will never forget it. But, if you oppose us, we will never forget it. And, after the war is over, we will destroy you and all your villages completely."

Despite such threats, Talabani remained reluctant to join Saddam's 'National Progressive Front'. Combined with his demands for oilfields around Kirkuk to be considered a part of Kurdistan (although that area was largely inhabited by Arabs and Turkomen), this became an insurmountable hurdle, and ultimately led to the collapse of the agreement, in 1985.

Meanwhile, a new player entered Iraq's Kurdish front when Barzani decided to capitalize upon Val Fajr-2 and seek support from his rival Talabani's sponsor – President Assad – who in turn was in dispute with Turkey over construction of a hydro-electric power scheme on the upper Euphrates. Assad, who was already supporting the PKK, decided Barzani could help put pressure upon Ankara by providing 'sanctuaries' for the PKK in northern Iraq. Barzani agreed and soon the PKK was striking into Turkey from its new bases. The furious Turks quickly concluded a joint security agreement with Iraq, on 20 April 1983, which granted them permission to enter Iraqi territory in so-called 'hot pursuit operations'. A suitable excuse for such incursions was available in the form of a major pipeline Iraq used to export its crude via Turkey – to pay for its war effort against Iran.[117]

The pipeline and the Oil Road, which ran parallel to it, were protected with barbed wire and a 15,000-strong force of Fursan. The installation was of obvious interest for Turkey, which was happy to accept cash from related construction contracts and transit fees – especially in exchange for Saddam's promises of joint action against the Kurds. Indeed, Turkey went a step further and depopulated the frontier region along a 25-kilometre strip, and created barriers to movement including wire entanglements, minefields and freefire zones to shield the Iraqi pipeline. Further protection was available in the form of 60,000 troops of VII Corps of the Turkish Army, part of the Malatya-based 2nd Army. The HQ of this corps delegated operations against the PKK to the Hakkari-based 3rd Infantry Division, which controlled no less than eight brigades: 2nd Commando, 5th Mountain Commando (often temporarily augmented by 1st Commando), 6th, 16th and 70th Mechanized, 6th Infantry, 23rd Security, and 34th Border. There were also two Jandarma (Gendarmerie) mobile brigades and a Special Operations battalion.

The first Turkish cross-border raid was undertaken from 25 to 29 May 1983, when two commando brigades launched a cordon-and-search operation near Dahuk. For the Peshmerga, which enjoyed several years of relative immunity, this came as a terrible shock, then in addition to the Iraqi pressure from the south, they were now facing Turkish forces in the north.

A second Turkish incursion followed on 25 August, and resulted in the capture, execution or imprisonment of many Iraqi Peshmerga. This instilled such Kurdish dread of Ankara, that when one of their splinter groups captured and held hostage two Turkish airmen who had crashed in northern Iraq, the hostages were returned to Turkey.

The threat also meant the Kurds tended to leave the oil pipeline untouched.

Meanwhile, Saddam's attention was focused upon the east. He was incensed at KDP participation in Val Fajr-2 and Val Fajr-4, which boosted Kurdish morale and secured safe supply lines to Barzani's forces. To hinder any expansion of the KDP, on 22-28 June 1983 Baghdad summoned all Kurds in the north born between 1963 and 1964 to report for military service. Furthermore, on 30 July 1983 Saddam's troops went through resettlement camps and villages around Arbil, arresting every man they could find, including members of the Fursan. Some 5,000-8,000 were then paraded through Baghdad and most were executed, with Saddam later observing: "They betrayed the country and they betrayed the covenant, and we meted out a stern punishment to them and they went to hell." The camps were then sealed off for a year with the families depending upon food being smuggled in.[118]

Meanwhile, Tehran urged the Barzanis to reinforce their forces in northern Iraq with their Peshmerga who had settled in Iran after 1975. The Barzani brothers were reluctant, fearing they were being pushed into a hostile environment before they were ready. Unsurprisingly, this led to a cooling of their relations with Tehran, where the clerics distrusted the secular and nationalist nature of the KDP. Nevertheless, Barazni's forces did support an attack by two Pasdaran brigades which advanced from Nowsud towards the Darban-i-Khan Dam in Feburary 1984.

Despite the ceasefire the PUK, or renegade elements within it, appear to have renewed operations against the Iraqis during the summer of 1984 – although other PUK units continued to fight alongside the Iraqi Army. Baghdad retaliated by deploying five divisions for an advance into PUK areas, razing several villages to the ground. This act strained relations between Talabani and Saddam but helped to shape events which broke the ceasefire – because, at the same time Tariq Aziz visited Ankara to sign another crossborder security agreement which now allowed Turkish forces to remain in Iraq for up to three days.[119]

The Turks promptly launched another cross-border offensive into Dahuk Province, leading Talabani to denounce the agreement as antiKurdish. His relations with Baghdad deteriorated rapidly, and resulted in a formal end to the ceasefire in January 1985. Fighting resumed with raids around the cities of Arbil and Kirkuk. Saddam's desperate last minute attempt to contain the Kurdish threat by offering an amnesty on 13 February 1985 was ignored by both the KDP and PUK.

The Kurdish Zenith, 1985-1987

Strengthened through control of the border area, the Kurds began deploying their forces closer to population centres. By May 1985, it was estimated that the Peshmerga controlled about a third of the Kurdish territory in Arbil, Dahuk, and Sulaymaniyah, while the Iraqis effectively controlled only the urban centres and oilfields.[120] By the autumn of 1986, the Iraqis lost further areas. The KDP, supplied through the Haj Umran Pass, controlled all of northern Dahuk and Arbil, and the 150-kilometre long section of the Turkish border. Similarly, the PUK – also supported by the Iranians – controlled most of the high ground of Sulaymaniyah Province, including the border territories south of Qalat Diza and as far west as Kirkuk.

The winter of 1985-1986 brought some respite for Iraq, although Iranian commandoes exploited growing Kurdish territorial control to mortar Sulaymaniyeh on 3 March 1986. The 45th Infantry Division staged a small counter-offensive from 25-30 April against the KDP around Shirwani Mazin, but its claims of success were overoptimistic. Barzani's Peshmerga soon began raiding along the Iraqi-Turkish pipeline, and on 15 May 1986 about 1,000 of them even took Mangezn (Mangesh or Mangezh) – a small garrison south-east of Zakhu – capturing some 800 defenders. An Iraqi counter-attack, spearheaded by a mountain brigade reinforced by Republican Guards, armour, Special Forces, Fursan and helicopter gunships, was ambushed and defeated on 19 May with another 800 prisoners taken.

The situation forced the Iraqi Army to rebuild its forces in

Kurdish militants with the wreckage of a downed Iraqi helicopter (including remnants of an UV-32-57 rocket pod). (Tom Cooper Collection)

45

The PUK invested heavily in creating the semblance of a conventional military. Here a group of its combatants during training on a 120mm mortar. (Albert Grandolini Collection)

Kurdish territory, establishing two divisional task forces; the 38th at Zakho (Zakhu) and 45th north of Arbil. These managed to recover Mangezn. However, Baghdad remained reliant upon 30,000 Turkish troops to protect the northern part of its pipeline, while the terrain along its south-eastern border prevented Ankara from successfully sealing it.

The Peshmerga's successes meant Iraqi maps showed signs of growing Kurdish sanctuaries. These were usually marked red even on official Iraqi maps, and described as 'areas Prohibited for Security Reasons' (or, more usually: 'Prohibited Areas'). All the inhabitants of these areas were considered hostile – even more so because communications in between such areas were subjected to frequent ambushes. The situation reached the point where Ali Hassan al-Majid later commented that it was impossible to travel from Kirkuk to Arbil, except in an armoured vehicle.[121]

The armament of the Peshmerga improved significantly during this period too. While initially armed with small arms and a few RPGs, they now obtained mortars and even some radios. The Peshmerga were professional fighters who received a small salary and usually served 15-20 days at a time, with equal spells at home to work their lands. They were augmented by many military-aged men (and some women) of the Civil Defense Force – a lightly armed militia.

There were differences between the two leading Kurdish resistance organizations. The KDP, which eventually had 15,000 Peshmerga and 30,000 militia, focused upon controlling the population; while the PUK, which grew to about 4,000 Peshmerga and 6,000 militia, seemed more interested in controlling territory and creating a conventional army. The KDP had dual military-political 'Branches': the 1st and 2nd in Arbil and Dahuk, and 3rd and 4th responsible for the Kirkuk area and Sulaymaniyah Province. The PUK had five sanctuaries in and around Sulaymaniyah, with its headquarters within the Jafati valley village of Yakhsamar, and four Regional Commands which were also responsible for military and political activity. The 1st and 2nd were responsible for operations in Sulaymaniyah Province, while the 3rd and 4th were active in neighbouring Balisan and Smaquli Valleys and responsible for operations in Arbil province.[122]

Smuggling was a way of life for the Kurds, who exploited the numerous pathways and goat trails to bring supplies and recruits from Iran. Supplies would be delivered to isolated buildings or caves for later distribution, sometimes using the ubiquitous Nissan Coaster pick-up truck, but Kurdish peasants were also encouraged

to store 10 per cent of their produce for the fighters. A captured Peshmerga told the Iraqis he and his friends had used a civilian vehicle to drive across the border all the way to Isfahan in central Iran – and back. They then infiltrated through the mountains without interruption and when asked how he had avoided the Iraqi line he asked: 'What line?'[123]

For the Iranians the rapprochement between the Barzanis and Talabani was a mixed blessing. Both were secular and nationalist, which aroused Iranian fears that success might encourage them to support their Iranian brothers. Therefore, Tehran sought a degree of control through a formal agreement with the two parties and encouraged closer co-operation between them. Geography strengthened Tehran's hand, for as Deputy PUK commander Naywshirwan Mustafa Amin noted: "There was no way for food and supplies to reach us, no help for our wounded, no roads out of the territory that we had liberated. Iran was our window to the world."[124]

Talabani sought a rapprochement with Tehran and in October 1986 they signed an agreement on economic, political and military cooperation leading Baghdad to call PUK-members 'Agents of Iran'. Meanwhile, Talabani and the Barzanis sought common ground for a future Kurdish state – a task eased by the death in January 1987 of Idris Barzani, leaving Masoud as undisputed KDP leader. The Kurdish factions then hammered out agreements for both political and national unity to provide a compromise acceptable to Iran between provincial autonomy and full independence. In February 1987 they created the Kurdistan National Front, and three months later a joint command. In early September they agreed to fight for a Kurdish state which would be in a confederation with a future democratic Iraq. This was acceptable to Tehran which steadily increased aid, and also forwarded Syrian supplies for the PUK, which together supported further Kurdish offensives. They continued to be allies with the Kurdish Socialist Party, which had 1,500 Peshmerga, and the Shia resistance Al Daawa. The latter would ultimately contribute to the Anfal catastrophe.

Fath Operations

Most operations involved interdicting traffic to erode enemy strength, gain equipment and dominate or control roads, as well as expanding 'sanctuaries' by controlling villages near the roads. But in 1986-1987 there were a series of offensives code-named Fath. Fath-2 struck Lake Dukan's hydro-electric facilities, while Fath-4 saw Iranian commandos and the KDP claiming to have destroyed an important air defence radar near Arbil. Fath-5 and Fath-7 aided Iranian army operations around Chwarta by attacking 27th Divisions' supply lines, and in a separate operation during May the PUK took Taqtaq, on the Kirkuk-Dukan Dam road, and held it for 10 hours. Fath-8 was staged around Atrush and the last operation, Fath-10 struck V Corps rear, and supply links for 33rd and 45th Divisions.

An increase in Kurdish activity in the Mawat sector, following Fath-1 and Fath-2, prompted the 39th Infantry Division to launch a month-long offensive starting on 7 November 1987. It claimed to have cleared 200 square kilometres allowing Iraqi engineers to build hard-topped roads.

Meanwhile, in September 1987, KDP forces took the Iraqi town of Kani Masi on the Turkish border, while combined PUK Iranian forces operating behind the Iraqi lines around Mawat took some 260 square kilometres of territory south of the Little Zab. In October the Iranian 67th Brigade, supported by some 2,000 PUK, made a mortar and MRLS attack upon the Kirkuk oil field, which they claimed

A column of PUK combatants moving between the mountains of north-eastern Iraq in 1987. (Albert Grandolini Collection)

A group of Pasdaran embarking a Toyota 4WD for a drive to the frontlines. The Iranians attempted to support several of operations run by Kurdish insurgents in north-eastern Iraq in 1987. (via N. S.)

reduced the flow of oil by 70 per cent. It appears to have had little effect, and by now 1.5 million BPD were flowing northwards.[125] Few of the Kurds were enthusiastic about fighting Iran's proxy war and especially against the pipeline which would provoke Turkish retaliation, so ceased their attacks upon the pipeline and focused upon fighting Saddam.

The Fath offensives would be the highpoint of the new Kurdish insurgency, aided by Operation Karbala-7 (see above), which further strengthened communications from Haj Umran. Tehran could be very satisfied with its Kurdish allies whose activities had even helped Operation Karbala-6 on the central front. These attacks resulted in US intelligence estimates from June 1987, in which the Kurds controlled 2,072 square kilometres of territory. In addition to

inflicting up to 2,000 casualties, they also brought in much booty, including about 100 mountain guns and recoilless rifles, 82mm and 120mm mortars, 107mm MRLS of Chinese origin, ZPU-4 quad anti-aircraft machineguns, SA-7 Strella MANPADS and even – in the case of the PUK – 11 T-55 MBTs.[126]

Kurdish fears of Turkish retaliation after the Iranian attacks upon the oil pipeline were well founded. In its campaign against the PKK and its Iraqi infrastructure, Ankara's 2nd Army maintained a fluctuating force of 12,000-20,000 men around the border, and in March 1987 they launched a major offensive against the PKK and, on 4 March, bombed Kurdish villages in Iraq.

Turkish concern about the PKK was increased by the deaths of 180 civilians and 260 Kurds between 1984 and 1986, leading to increased pressure on the Kurds both in Turkey and Iraq. Ankara revealed in November 1986 that its troops had twice crossed the border in hot pursuit of Kurdish guerrillas, and there had also been 20 crossborder air attacks.

Turkey's secular Moslem regime was also acutely sensitive to the activities of the Iranian theocrats. Following Karbala-7 it notified Tehran that it would not permit the capture of the Kirkuk and Mosul oilfields, emphasising the point by bombing Kurdish villages in Iraq, which led to Rafsanjani's hasty visit to Ankara, and adopting a conciliatory approach as described above.

Yet the Ramadan Headquarters continued to direct Kurdish operations, with the Fath offensives followed by the Zafar (Triumph or Victory – in Arabic and Farsi) series, starting on 15 August 1987 and continuing until mid-March 1988. These claimed a number of significant successes; Zafar-2 saw the Kifri defences penetrated, while Zafar-3 was a pre-emptive attack upon 36th Infantry Division as it prepared to strike the Qara Dagh ridge. Zafar-4 damaged the electricity network in the town of Dahuk.[127]

There would be three operations during 1988, beginning with the wide-ranging Zafar-5. This overran the bases of 38th Infantry Division and three NDB battalions around Kani Masi on the Turkish border, and took the road bridge near al-Amadiyah. It also led to the downing of a Su-22 and the capture of its pilot (1st Lieutenant Ali Hameed al-Jabouri of No 109 Squadron was shot down on 15 January but his subsequent fate is unknown).[128] Zafar-6 disrupted traffic at the crossroads town of Sangaw; while Zafar-7 was undertaken in support of the Iranian Operation Val Fajr-10 and claimed to have destroyed 423rd Infantry Brigade, from 43rd Infantry Division, during attacks on Khurmal.

Table 7: The 'Fath' Offensives (October 1986-September 1987)				
Operation	Began	Provinces	Kurds	Other
Fath 1	10.10.86 (to 13.10.86)	Arbil, Sulamaniyah	PUK	66 Bde IRGC
Fath 2	29.10.86	Sulamaniyah	PUK	75 Bde IRGC
Fath 3	14.11.86 (to 19.11.87)	Dahuk	KDP	75 Bde IRGC
Fath 4	11.3.87 (to 22.2.87)	Arbil, Sulamaniyah	KDP	75 Bde IRGC
Fath 5	14.4.87 (to 20.4.87)	Sulamaniyah	PUK	75 Bde IRGC
Fath 6	17.6.87 (to 28.6.87)	Arbil	KDP	75 Bde IRGC
Fath 7	17.6.87 (to 28.6.87)	Sulamaniyah	PUK	75 Bde IRGC
Fath 8	19.7.87	Dahuk	KDP	75 Bde IRGC
Fath 9	9.8.87	Sulaymaniyah	PUK	75 Bde IRGC
Fath 10	3.9.87 (to 5.9.87)	Arbil	KDP	75 Bde, Daawa

Baghdad strikes back

With Iraq's red-white-black banner flying only over the larger population centres, by 1987 it was clear radical changes were required in counter-insurgency policy. Counter-insurgency was a joint responsibility between the corps commanders and the Ba'ath Party's Northern Bureau in Kirkuk – initially under Sa'adi Mahdi Saleh and then Muhammad Hamza al-Zubeidi (responsible for a population of 3,760,244, of whom 2,064,712 were Kurds).[129] The Army deployed about half-a-dozen infantry brigades, and a similar number of commando/special forces brigades, with some 30,000 men, augmented by some nine Border Guard brigades (18,000 troops), who reverted to their own command in March 1985 but remained under Army operational control.[130]

The backbone of counter-insurgency remained the Kurdish NDBs which scouted, escorted convoys, manned road blocks, patrolled in the countryside or were transported to remote bases by helicopter. As Kurds they were familiar with the usual hiding places, and usually conducted searches of homes and farms, and captured suspects who were turned over to the authorities.

Much of the Iraqi COIN effort remained passive and reactive. A blockade with fortified check points was established around each Kurdish sanctuary area, where people, animals, and vehicles were searched to prevent them from importing food and medicine. Usually only women were permitted to move between the zones.[131]

Along the roads, and around the cities and towns, were fortified bases from which convoy escorts, and reaction forces to assist smaller beleaguered bases or convoys under attack, would depart. Many of these were brick or concrete structures surrounded by sandbags and barbed wire, but at Nizarkeh in the eastern suburb of Dohuk, was a huge concrete structure – built to Soviet design in the 1970s – protected by a battery of four anti-aircraft guns mounted on the roof. Some sites were fire-bases which divided prohibited areas into target zones which might be shelled at any time. However, even the biggest guns in the Iraqi arsenal had a limited reach.[132]

Although Iraqi documents indicate the GMID exploited the fractious nature of Kurdish political and tribal relations to enrol many agents, and they produced abundant intelligence, it was little used. There were no major attempts to penetrate the 'sanctuaries'; retaliatory actions struck easy targets near the roads, with buildings demolished and the surviving inhabitants transferred to resettlement camps close to military bases. Helicopters were used by commandos, Special Forces and Kurdish Special Units for raids into enemy territory, against headquarters and supply dumps, to lay mines along Kurdish infiltration routes, or for infantry and Fursan search operations looking for supply dumps; but the men rarely stayed overnight.

The deterioration in Iraqi security occurred under Zubeidi, who appears to have replaced Saleh sometime in 1984. As the Kurds grew bolder there was a full scale review in about March 1986, and Zubeidi was told to turn the situation around within six months. Yet despite the lack of improvement he was given another six months, by which time the security situation had reached a nadir. His failure influenced Saddam's decision to make radical changes; a decision also influenced by the presence of the Shia resistance movement, Al Daawa, in Kurdistan where it claimed 1,000 of its members were active. Another factor was KDP and PUK support for Karbala-7, with Talabani talking of seceding from Iraq, but the fuse was lit with success on the Basra front where the Iranian offensive Karbala 5 was defeated in March (see Volume 3).[133]

Chemical Ali

Saddam had long supported the policy of 'active defence' in conventional operations (partly to offset the Iranian war of attrition), and now he wished this policy to apply against the Kurds. On 15 March 1987, after Karbala-7, he presided over a five-hour meeting of the Armed Forces General Command, which was attended by his cousin Ali Hassan al-Majid – a member of the Regional Command of the Ba'ath Party and President of the General Security Office – dubbed 'Chemical Ali'. Former head of the General Security Directorate (Amn), he was described as being of use when Saddam needed somebody without a heart, and is known to have had some success against the Kurds in Sulaymaniyah in October 1985.[134]

Saddam (like Hitler) always admired ruthlessness, which he equated with effectiveness, and on 18 March 1987 the Revolutionary Command Council and the Ba'ath Party's Regional Command jointly appointed Majid as new head of the Ba'ath Northern Bureau. Within a fortnight he was granted extraordinary powers, 'for the purpose of protecting security and order, safeguarding stability, and applying autonomous rule in the region'. His decisions were mandatory for all state agencies, military, civilian and security – including the GMID and the Popular Army.

Majid was well briefed about the situation and later told aides he gave himself two years to succeed. He began publishing decrees, directives and orders; clearly showing he intended not only to destroy the Kurdish resistance but to crush those Kurds who refused to accept Iraqi rule. He would later tell a court: "I am the one who gave orders to the army to demolish villages and relocate villagers. The army was responsible for carrying out those orders, I am not defending myself. I am not apologising."

Majid at first lacked the resources to implement his plans, but one of his earliest decisions was to double the number of NDBs which were placed under operational control of the GMID-controlled 1st National Defence Headquarters, and warned '...we will push you to your target until you all get killed.[135]'

Majid waited only for the spring thaw to begin his new policy with a three-phase operation in 1987 against PUK which he described as

Table 8: The Zafar offensives, August 1987-March 1988

Operation	Began	Provinces	Kurds	Other
Zafar 1	15.8.87 (to 18.9.87)	Dahuk	KDP	75 Bde, Daawa
Zafar 2	5.10.87 (to 7.10.87)	At-Tamin, Diyala	PUK	75 Bde, Daawa
Zafar 3	5.10.87 (to 17.11.87)	Sulaymaniyah	PUK	75 Bde
Zafar 4	20.11.87	Dahuk	KDP	75 Bde
Zafar 5	13.1.88 (to 17.1.88)	At-Tamin, Dahuk, Diyala	KDP	75 Bde
Zafar 6	24.2.88	At-Tamin, Sulaymaniyah	PUK	75 Bde, Daawa
Zafar 7	13.3.88	Sulaymaniyah	PUK	75 Bde, Daawa

'village collectivisation'. An ominous feature of this plan was the use of chemical weapons – which would earn Majid the nickname of 'Chemical Ali' (Ali Kimyawi) – and for which he was hanged in January 2010 having been convicted of eight capital crimes. He readily admitted the use of chemical weapons commenting:

I will kill them all with chemical weapons. Who is going to say anything? The international community? Fuck them!

However he was not alone: Saddam had discussed the idea that the IrAF use its 'special arsenal' (chemical weapons) against Kurdish headquarters and bases, and Defence Minister General Adnan Khairallah Talfah (Khairallah) suggested 'Whatever we cannot defeat, we should use special ammunition to secure areas'. Unsurprisingly, there are reports that the Iraqis used chemical weapons against the Kurds around Haj Umran starting already on 18 August 1983.[136]

The use of air power against the Kurds was as old as modern Iraq – which the British controlled during the 1920s and early 1930s, through 'air policing'. A Turkish incursion around Rawandiz, and post war defence cuts, led to the decision that the Royal Air Force (RAF) would be used in an aerial policing role, predominantly against the Kurds. The Colonial Secretary, Winston Churchill, and the RAF Chief-of-Staff, Sir Hugh Trenchard, discussed the use of chemical weapons against the Kurds, but did not put this policy into practice. Churchill noted on 17 August 1921, 'The only weapons which can be used by the Air Force are bombs and machine guns'. In addition to 98.5 tonnes of high-explosive bombs, the British deployed those filled with phosphorus too.[137]

Possibly influenced by Turkish cross-border operations, all of Majid's offensives would follow a pattern in which he would 'lasso' a Prohibited Area using commando/Special Forces – to cordon the remoter areas – and conventional forces exploiting the road networks. He would then draw the 'noose' tight to capture the majority of the inhabitants and transfer them to resettlement camps, raze their villages and farms to the ground and often take away most of the adult males (including young teens and old men) for interrogation, often followed by execution. But occasionally NDB commanders, and more rarely Iraqi officers, would take pity on the wretched Kurds and save their lives. The NDBs were more interested in loot, including livestock, cash, gold, watches, as well as rugs, mattresses and blankets, picture albums and even toothpaste!

Majid's 'Collectivisation'

Plans for the 'collectivisation' were published on 13 April 1987 by V Corps' Lieutenant General Khalil Ibrahim Talia al-Durri (Talia al-Durri). Phase I (21 April – 20 May 1987) and Phase II (21 May-20 June 1987) would assault the PUK 'sanctuaries' with the General Security Directorate (Amn) to prepare deeper penetrations in a later Phase III. Truck-loads of explosives were assembled to ensure that no Kurdish villages would remain standing, while 200 civilian bulldozers were commandeered, and any officer who left even a wall standing would have to return to finish the job. Wells were to be filled in, electricity cables were to be ripped out and the area left so that no farming could be carried out.[138]

The first phases were clearly preparatory and focused upon villages near the major roads east of Mosul, even those already under government control with Fursan garrisons, as well as the smaller road networks within the 'sanctuaries.' Stringent restrictions were imposed on all grain sales in the region and upon the transport of food between the provinces. The offensive was heralded by chemical weapon attacks on the PUK heartland of the Jafati valley and the 2nd

and 3rd Malabands on 15 April; possibly in retaliation for a renewed PUK offensive, but it helped put the Peshmerga on the back foot. They had anticipated chemical weapon attacks and suffered few casualties but failed to warn the civilians, of whom some 400 died. In the next few months chemical weapons were delivered into the valley and its neighbours by gun, MLRS, high-speed combat aircraft and the Pilatus light attack aircraft.

On 21 April 1987 Majid's plan went into effect all over Kurdistan, with 661 villages affected; 219 around Arbil, 122 in the Germain, and 320 throughout Sulaymaniyah Province, token compensation sometimes being offered to families of the 200,000 displaced. The campaign ended on 20 June, and aircraft then periodically flew over the affected areas to extinguish activity once detected. While Saddam and Majid felt they had made a good start – having cleared the main roads from Mosul-Arbil-Kirkuk-Tuz Khurmatu, and from the Darband-i-Khan dam to Kalar and the road network around Kifri – they were not completely satisfied. Some army officers were shocked at the brutality of the orders, indeed Talia al-Durri reportedly refused to destroy some of the villages fearing these actions would only stiffen resistance. The relocation effort was poorly managed, inadequately funded, and was extremely discriminatory while some resettlement camps did not exist.

With conventional operations now absorbing much of the Army's energies and resources, Majid had to focus upon administrative action to maintain pressure upon the Kurds. On 3 June he informed I, II and V Corps, and intelligence and counter-intelligence organizations, that all human activity was banned in 1,000 Kurdish villages, and those aged 15-70 who failed to show allegiance to the regime would be shot together with their animals. On 20 June he sanctioned Fursan pillaging of villages, and from 29 September tightened the screw by reducing food rations for Kurdish civilians outside the 'sanctuaries' to the bare minimum. The blockade of those areas was tightened, with greater vigilance at check points, shutting Kurdish grocery stores and carefully monitored stocks at restaurants, bakeries and cafes. A planned national census for 17 October was also 'weaponised'; for those whose names were not included were deemed hostile to the regime, although many in the remoter areas were totally unaware it was being conducted.[139]

The Kurdish reaction to Majid's 'collectivisation' was a new series of raids, and the PUK's 2nd Malaband struck out of the Jafati Valley in mid-April, overrunning dozens of outposts.[140] This and the increasing use of Daawa troops strengthened Majid's case for more resources, but he pressed on with those he had, and his success meant that in the wake of Iraqi victories on the Basra front in Operations 'Ramadan Mubarak' and 'Tawakkalna ala Allah (1)' (see Volume 3) the improved strategic situation allowed Saddam to provide the resources for the murderous Anfal campaigns. He observed at a meeting sometime in June or July 1988 "That will teach (the Kurds) a painful lesson; so next time before they think to raise the issue against us they will think twice as they remember the pain that they have suffered in this lesson".[141]

Anfal Campaigns

The offensives took their name – an-Anfal – from the 8th Sura of the Koran, which refers to the 'spoils of war' which are due to the righteous from the infidel once they are driven them from their land. The prime target would be Talabani's PUK, which would suffer seven of the eight offensives, for a variety of reasons including its 1985 'betrayal', its proximity both to the front and key communications routes, as well as its high physical profile occupying key valleys and uplands.[142]

The decision to begin the campaign was apparently taken by Saddam at a meeting in February 1988 attended by Defence Minister Khairallah, Chief-of-Staff Lieutenant General Nizar Abdel Karim General Nizar Abdel Karim and brigades are Alwiya. s been disputed. It is retained here for ease of recognition.al-Khazraji, GMID head Saber Abd al-Aziz and, of course, Majid. The Army assigned the initial operation to I Corps under Major General Sultan Hashim Ahmed al-Tai, who had just been transferred from VI Corps (on 3 March 1991 Hashim would negotiate the terms of the ceasefire after 'Desert Storm'). Majid's strategy focused upon the PUK 'sanctuaries' which could support Iranian army operations, and were also targeted because they were more visible and easier to access from surrounding road systems. He intended to burn out the heart of PUK resistance, working his way clockwise through their central Sulaymaniyah 'sanctuaries' and then finish off the northernmost.

Intelligence of a PUK plan to take the Lake Dukan Dam made the PUK headquarters in the Jafati valley the first target, and Hashim was given operational control of the V Corps 4th Mountain and 33rd Infantry Divisions, which would attack from the north, while his own 24th Infantry Division and 1st Commando Brigade struck from the south.

Anfal-1

The Peshmerga within the Jafati valley did not fear chemical weapons as they were equipped gas masks and atropine injectors, and MANPADS for defence against enemy aircraft. However, this made them complacent while the departure of Talabani in a vain attempt to gain support from Washington meant his deputy, Naywshirwan Mustafa Amin, was in charge. Before dawn on 23 February the PUK positions came under artillery and MLRS bombardment, and at dawn I Corps pushed northward and east, as V Corps drove south. PUK forces were able to delay them for three weeks until 18 March, when they retreated eastward through a corridor left open by the Iraqis as an escape route.

Anfal-2

A sense of urgency was brought to the 'Anfal' operations by the Iranian offensive around Halabja (Val Fajr-10), and the Iraqis feared the enemy were trying to reach the Qara Dagh 'sanctuary' to create a massive enclave which would threaten Sulaymaniyah.[143] They launched Anfal-2 on 22 March south of the Chamchamal-Sulaymaniyeh highway around Qara Dagh, and cut the lines of communications to PUK forces threatening the Kirkuk area. The defenders were the PUK's 1st Malaband, some Iraqi Communists and up to 400 Pasdaran who had dispersed for fear of chemical attack. The attack was directed by Major General Iyad Khalil Zaki, who was assigned the 43rd Division Task Force and 28th Infantry Division – both of which had to leave substantial forces on the eastward-facing front – as well as three Special Force brigades (65th, 66th and 68th) and the 1st National Defence Headquarters. The offensive opened with MLRS launching chemically-tipped rockets; these panicked the civilian population who fled, soon followed by the Peshmerga, and by 1 April the operation was over.

Anfal-3

Following another brief pause the Iraqis continued their campaign into the Germain. It appears a scratch force of elements from I Corps was put together under Special Forces officer Brigadier General Bareq Abdullah al-Haj Hunta, with the new 50th Division Task Force controlling three infantry brigades (417th, 443rd, 444th),

and three Special Forces brigades (65th, 66th, 68th) as well as the 1st National Defence Headquarters and Emergency Forces (the general would be executed in 1991 for the hasty and chaotic withdrawal from Kuwait). The open countryside was not good guerrilla country, but the remnants of 1st Malaband had little choice but to defend the area as it was main recruiting ground for the PUK Peshmergas.

The offensive began on 7 April and appears to have omitted the usual chemical screen, possibly because the open ground was suitable for mechanized forces to cross quickly. Qadir Karam fell on 10 April. The exhausted Peshmerga were short of supplies and faced; overwhelming force caused morale to collapse and many surrendered, and although one or two groups held out for five days the campaign concluded on 20 April.

Anfal-4

Having purged the area south of the Kirkuk-Sulaymaniyah highway, Hashim and Majid now looked north. The valley of the Lesser Zab around Taqtaq had been briefly held by PUK a year earlier. At a meeting on 13 April the PUK leaders decided the Peshmerga would retreat, taking the surviving civilians north of the Kirkuk-Sulaymaniyah highway. One column, led by 1st Malband headed for Askar in the Lesser Zab valley to set up a new base.

Shortly after their arrival, a chemical attack by the IrAF at dusk on 3 May caused general panic and confusion. A force of Iraqi troops, including 10th Armoured (reinforced with two infantry brigades) and 46th Infantry Divisions, with I Corps' 1st Commando Brigade and three Special Forces brigades (65th, 66th and 68th), plus Fursan, attacked at dawn on 4 May. There was little prolonged resistance, but at one point Hashim had to bring in some 700 Emergency Force troops by helicopter. Many Peshmerga escaped northward in carts drawn by commandeered tractors, and by 8 May the fighting was over and 138 Kurdish villages were abandoned. Up to a third of the population, many of them women and children, had disappeared.

Anfal 5-7

The destruction of the PUK was almost complete, and its remnants filed into Iraq's northeast Arbil Province to hold the Balisan valley, running the gauntlet of 24th and 39th Infantry Divisions west of Lake Dukan. The rugged valley was defended by PUK 3rd Malband, the Socialist Party of Kurdistan, Iraqi Communists and some KDP. They began to stockpile food and ammunition in anticipation of a prolonged struggle.

The I Corps was again responsible for mopping up the last PUK resistance and committed 23rd, 24th and 39th Infantry Divisions, four commando/Special Forces brigades and the ubiquitous Fursan. There were few civilians in the region as many had fled from the sustained gas attacks that had begun in May 1987 and were renewed at dusk on 15 May. Following a week-long lull the IrAF launched a sustained chemical assault from 23 May.

The initial assault on 16 May took 20 villages, but encountered fierce resistance and petered out inconclusively by 7 June. The V Corps' Brigadier General Yunis Muhammad al-Zareb was now authorized to complete clearance of the valley in two simultaneous operations, 'Anfal 6 and 7.' Plans for the operations were drawn up by V Corps as early as 30 May, but Khazraji General Nizar Abdel Karim and brigades are Alwiya. s been disputed. It is retained here for ease of recoordered a postponement pending the outcome of Tawakkalna ala Allah-2, which would be launched on 25 June 1988 (see Volume 3). Only on 23 June did Saddam authorise the next stage, but a postponement was ordered on 29 June to build up resources. On

20 July Khazraji stated the operation had been postponed until after the Feast of 'Id al-Adha (i.e after 25 July), possibly because on 17 July Iranian President Ali Khamenei notified the United Nations that he was willing to accept UN Security Council Resolution 598. Two days earlier Rafsanjani had announced Iran's intention to withdraw its forces in Iraq and began to do so the following day. These announcements were a shock for the PUK because they regarded it as breaching the October 1986 Teheran agreement; this had stipulated that neither party would make a unilateral deal with Baghdad. Iran accepted Iraqi terms for a ceasefire on 8 August.

On 26 July the Peshmerga decided to conduct a partial withdrawal behind a rear-guard. As this began the IrAF began a new campaign, using chemical weapons, to drive the Peshmerga up the mountains and cluster bombs to drive them down. On 26 or 27 August the remaining Peshmerga contingents in the Balisan Valley fled. The ceasefire with Iran was announced on August 7. I Corps, however, continued mopping-up operations until 26 August.

Anfal-8

The remoteness of the KDP's 'sanctuary' in the Badinan valley, and the difficult surrounding terrain, meant that this was the last 'Anfal' target. The offensive was authorised on 28 July, and planning was completed on 16 August. Assembling the resources took time; in a letter to Saddam on 7 August, an impatient Majid urged him to finish the KDP, but the following day the ceasefire with Iran was announced.

The KDP claimed it had 8,000 Peshmerga and 36,000 militia. Iraqi intelligence put KDP Peshmerga strength at 2,600, augmented by up to 300 PUK Peshmerga, 220 Iraqi Communists, and some 70 Kurdistan Popular Democratic Party (a KDP breakaway group). To ensure success the 38th and 45th Infantry Divisions were joined by 29th and 41st Infantry Divisions, transferred from VI Corps following Tawakkalna ala Allah-2, to give 16 brigades including four of commando/Special Forces. Each division organized two task forces with strong Fursan support; the 29th Infantry Division alone controlling 16 NDBs.[144] Some 100,000 men supported by up to 500 guns and overwhelming air power helped to ensure success, but the commanders had to be careful not to provoke the Turks. Formidable engineering resources had to be assembled both to support the advance and to destroy up to 400 villages.

The IrAF was responsible for deploying chemical weapons, reportedly mustard gas and Sarin nerve gas, during this offensive but it also made extensively use of 'iron' and cluster bombs. The chemical weapons were used not only against individual KDP bases but also against some 49 villages – with aircraft reportedly covering strips 60 miles wide and 20 miles deep – causing panic among both civilians and Peshmerga whose morale broke as they tried to save their relatives.

The Iraqi advance involved (west-to-east) 38th, 29th, 41st and 45th Divisions with a large number of tank, artillery and MLRS battalions in support. This advance met scattered resistance, which largely ended by dusk on 26 August when Barzani apparently ordered his fighters to cease resistance, although some ignored the order. The last shots were fired on the border on 6 September, and that afternoon, to Majid's fury, Iraqi radio announced "a general and comprehensive amnesty for all Iraqi Kurds...both inside and outside of Iraq" with the exception of Talabani.[145] The security forces lost 31 dead, including 18 Fursan, and captured 13,395 Kurds, including 1,574 Peshmerga. This figure included 3,063 men – many of whom were executed – who were deemed part of the Kurdish resistance ('saboteurs'). Even villages that had once been regarded as loyal suffered, many because they did not participate in the 1987 census: their failure was regarded as evidence of the deepest treason.

The 'Anfal' campaigns reportedly involved 14 infantry divisions and two Guards divisions which, with other forces, totalled 250,000 men, or 33 per cent of the Iraqi ground forces. It is worth noting that they also allowed the Turkish Army to put pressure upon the PKK. It is claimed that the campaigns destroyed more than 4,000 villages, displaced a million people and caused 182,000 to disappear.[146] Yet within three years, Kurdish resistance was reignited following the Coalition's Operation 'Desert Storm' and quickly carved out a fully autonomous region, under Barzani, recognized by Baghdad in 2005. That same year, in an act of tremendous irony, Talabani, who had been denied amnesty "...because of his wilful and repeated violations of law and order, even after he was granted opportunities to reform his ways" – become Iraq's president and remained so until a stroke forced him to resign in 2014. He refused to sign death warrants for Majid, who had been sentenced to death together with Hashim, and while the former would pay the ultimate penalty, the general had his sentence commuted to 15 years of imprisonment.

CHAPTER 7
THE LAST BATTLES 1988

The general lull on the Central Front lasted some 18 months, with the focus of operations during the spring of 1988 switching to the Northern Front and Iran's Operation Beit-ol- Mogaddas-5. As late as 26 May Saddam, who was worried by enemy progress on the Northern Front, was determined the Central Front would remain on the defensive, rejecting even a IV Corps proposal for an advance in the Tib sector to improve the line. The Guards, he said, could contain any local Iranian threat and line adjustment would consume, rather than release, troops.[147]

In June he changed his mind as he recognized that the recapture of the Majnoon bridgehead in the Tawakkalna ala Allah-2 offensive meant Tehran had lost all the ground it had won since 1982, and was in a desperate situation. The Iranian ground forces, especially

the Pasdaran, were utterly demoralized, with the mere threat of gas attack capable of causing panic, and they lacked the means to resist having lost vast amounts of equipment. When Saddam met his commanders on 27 June, Khazraji, backed by Khairallah, proposed targeting the IRIA to prevent a post-war threat, the Defence Minister noting the lightly-equipped Pasdaran would achieve nothing without IRIA support.[148]

Saddam agreed as part of a strategy of clearing 'the Persians' from Iraqi territory in three stages; a IV Corps thrust to push back the enemy on the Tib-Fakkeh front and secure Amarah, then I and V Corps would remove the enemy enclave around Mawat, and finally II Corps would strike in the Sanuba and Saif Saad Plateaus between Sumar and Mehran. The objective of the next stage, Operation

Tawakkalna ala Allah-3, was to smash the enemy south of Dehloran.

Operation Tawakkalna ala Allah-3

The plan envisaged one heavy blow around the hotly-contested town of Fakkeh and a second around Tib. The northern part of the battlefield would be in the area of the Abu al-Gharb Plateau, which overlooked the River Doveyrich. This 1-5 metre-deep river provided a 10-15-metre-wide shield running southwards in an undulating plain criss-crossed with river valleys.

Detailed planning began on 27 June and was based upon two offensives; by IV Corps in the north and the Guards Corps in the south. IV Corps, now under Major General Iyad Khlil Zaki, had seven divisions to attack northeastwards around Tib and Abu Ghirab, with 29th and 20th Infantry Divisions breaking through in the first phase to seize the high ground and aid the recapture of Iraqi territory to the Doveyrich. This would also allow 1st and 5th Mechanized Divisions to push into enemy territory supported by two armoured and two commando brigades, as well as 2nd Infantry Division. The 18th and 32nd Infantry Divisions would be in reserve and the corps would be supported by seven engineer battalions as well as 34 artillery battalions (612 guns and MLRS) and a FROG battalion.

The Guards under Lieutenant General Iyad Futaykh Khalifa al-Rawi would have the Medina Manarwah Armoured, Baghdad Infantry, Nebuchadnezzar Mixed, and Special Operations Divisions deployed between Abu Ghirab Plateau and Fakkeh to drive eastwards. Medina was to swing north up the road towards Musiyan before taking the road east through Eyn Kush and Dasht-e Abbas, targeting enemy reserves, artillery concentrations and headquarters. It would also relieve a Special Forces battalion of 16th Special Forces Brigade of the Republican Guards Corps in the Eyn-e Kush area to isolate the battlefield. The corps had some 200 MBTs and an artillery train of 20 gun and MLRS battalions (360 tubes and MLRS) together with a FROG battalion. The two corps would be supported by the 4th IrAAC Wing with 140 helicopters, including 40 gunships, while the IrAF would provide 150 aircraft in six CAS and one air defence squadrons augmented by electronic jamming and photo reconnaissance detachments.[149]

The defences were largely under the IRIA's SFOHQ and as 16th Armoured Division had moved north to cover the Mehran sector this left the Guards and IV Corps facing the 21st and 77th IRIA Infantry Divisions respectively, each of two brigades. They were augmented by a brigade each of 84th Infantry and 23rd Special Forces Divisions IRIA, and Pasdaran, together with Gendarmerie supported by 55th Artillery Group with 21 artillery battalions (the 21st Division's 2nd Brigade and probably 77th Division's 3rd Brigade were not with their parent units). The defences exploited the natural strength of the western foothills of the Jebel Hamrin, while in the south there were berms and deep minefields, the defenders having six brigades in the front line and two in reserve.

The artillery preparation on 12 July began at 06:45 and as usual was short; lasting only 30 minutes. The assault began in challenging conditions with intense heat (45° C) and high winds which created sand storms in the south. But this did not prevent the Guards completing Phase One by 11:00 using four infantry and a commando brigade as the defence collapsed, allowing the exploitation to begin. The mechanized forces quickly reached the River Doveyrich by 13:00 and, aided by the Guards Special Forces, seized the bridges. Other Special Forces were flown 12 kilometres inside Iran to Musa al-Khawi, using 40 helicopters, and they held until relieved by 2nd Armoured Brigade of Medina Guards Division at 16:00 hours. IV

IRGC troops in the mountains around the Abu Ghirab Plateau in early 1988. (via N. S.)

By 1988 the IRGC operated a small artillery unit equipped with 2S1 Gvozdika self-propelled 122mm howitzers. Here one is seen in action on the front near Dehloran. (via N. S.)

Corps was similarly successful attacking on a 60-kilometre front and completing Phase One in 75 minutes. Phase Two was completed two hours later at 10:30 and by 16:00 it controlled Musiyan, in operations greatly aided by the IrAAC.

The success excited Saddam who kept moving from one corps headquarters to the other, and he now ordered the Guards to send 2nd Armoured Brigade of the Medina Division south to Chananeh to overrun the sector headquarters. Meanwhile Nebuchadnezzar was to send a mechanised brigade, and Baghdad an armoured brigade, to secure arms dumps. The units moved out at dawn on 13 July and by midday had secured their objectives against slight resistance. Around the same time, IV Corps was ordered to send 5th Mechanized Division to take Dehloran, which the enemy had abandoned, and it did so during the morning of 13 July.

Advances of up to 45 kilometres left Iraq briefly in control of some 400 square kilometres of Iranian territory, including Dehloran, but Saddam was no longer interested in seizing ground; only in destroying Tehran's means of continuing the war. On 13 July 1988 he threatened to invade southern Iran if the Iranians did not abandon their Kurdistan enclaves including Halabjah. With Iran now down to an estimated 200 tanks and short of military equipment, the next day Rajsanjani announced that all Iranian forces would withdraw from occupied Iraqi territory north of Haj Umran, the last major piece of Iraqi territory which they held.[150] In the south the Iraqis mopped up, and on the afternoon of 15 July withdrew, taking 5,000-7,000 prisoners and military booty including 90 MBTs, 60 APC/ICVs and 130 guns.

Tawakkalna ala Allah-4

On 18 July 1988, the 20th anniversary of Ba'ath rule, Saddam Hussein again called for peace negotiations and claimed Iraq had no territorial claims. He warned that he would not give the Iranians time to rebuild their forces and would continue to attack economic targets. Iran faced enemy victories and heavy losses, a growing fear

Table 9: Order of Battle for Operation Tawakkalna ala Allah-4, July 1988		
Corps	**Division**	**Brigades**
Iraq		
Republican Guards Corps	Corps troops; Artillery Brigade Republican Guards Corps	
	Baghdad Guards Infantry Division	9th Armoured Brigade; 14th Mechanised Brigade; 4th & 7th Infantry Brigades, 21st Commando Guards Brigades
	Guards Special Operations Division	15th & 18th Mechanised Brigades; 3rd & 16th Special Forces Guards Brigades
	Hammurabi Guards Armoured Division	8th Armoured, 29th Mechanised, 5th Infantry Guards Brigades
	Medina Manarwah Guards Armoured Division	2nd & 10th Armoured, 6th Infantry Guards Brigades
	Nebuchadnezzar Guards Mixed Division	17th Armoured; 11th & 12th Commando; 22nd & 23rd Infantry Guards Brigades
	1st Wing IrAAC	
II Corps	Corps troops; II Corps Commando Brigade; II Corps Special Forces Brigade	
	5th Mechanised Division	26th Armoured; 15th & 20th Mechanised; 505th Infantry Brigades
	10th Armoured Division	17th & 42nd Armoured; 24th Mechanised Brigades
	16th Infantry Division	99th & 604th Infantry Brigades
	17th Armoured Division	59th & 70th Armoured; 99th Mechanised Brigades
	21st Infantry Division	59th Armoured; 90th, 423rd, 430th, 706th Infantry Brigades
	22nd Infantry Division	70th Armoured; 93rd, 425th, 706th Infantry Brigades
	28th Infantry Division	78th, 412th, 417th Infantry Brigades
	2nd Wing IrAAC	
I Special Corps	10th Commando Brigade; IV Corps Commando Brigade; I Special Corps Artillery Brigade	
	1st Special Infantry Division	1st, 2nd, 3rd Infantry Brigades
	2nd Special Infantry Division	4th, 5th, 6th Infantry Brigades
	3rd Special Infantry Division	7th, 8th, 9th Infantry Brigades
	12th Armoured Division	50th Armoured Brigade
	unk. Infantry Brigade	
Iran		
Northern Forward Operational Headquarters		
	16th Armoured Division IRIA	1st, 2nd, 3rd Armoured Brigades
	58th Infantry Division IRIA	1st, 2nd, 3rd Infantry Brigades
	81st Armoured Division IRIA	1st, 2nd, 3rd Armoured; 4th Mechanized Brigades
	84th Infantry Division IRIA	1st, 2nd, 3rd Infantry Brigades
	88th Armoured Division IRIA	1st, 2nd, 3rd Armoured Brigades
	37th Armoured Brigade IRIA	
	55th Airborne Brigade IRIA	
	127th Meghdad Infantry Brigade IRGC	
	33rd Artillery Group IRIA	
	44th Artillery Group IRIA	
	1st & 3rd CSG, 4th GSG IRIAA	

of chemical weapons and attacks on her cities, threats from Western naval power and diplomatic isolation.

The previous day Iran's President Khameini wrote to the UN Secretary General, Javier Perez de Cueller, requesting a ceasefire and accepting UN Resolution 598. According to one press report the decision was reached in an eighthour meeting between Khomeini and some 40 of his leading officials and commanders. The deciding factor was the statement by the Pasdaran commander Mohsen Rezai

that the war could be won only after another five years of conflict. In fact the country was nearly bankrupt, having used up most of its foreign reserves, and its industry was on the verge of collapse. The currency was almost worthless and oil markets were turning to other producers. Moreover the regime itself was becoming unpopular and this threatened the revolution.

But Iraq refused to accept the initial Iranian cease-fire proposal, claiming the Iranian acceptance was ambiguous for Khomeini had not publicly indicated he would agree to a cease-fire. Also Saddam Hussein refused to accept continued Iranian mobilisation. He underlined his point by a series of air attacks upon Iranian industrial targets. This forced Iran to appeal to the UN Security Council, but on 20 July Khomeini himself issued a public statement accepting the cease-fire. He said: "Taking this decision was more deadly than taking poison. I submitted myself to God's will and drank this drink for his satisfaction (Lessons p.395.)."

Saddam remained anxious to exploit the successes of the first three 'Tawakkalna ala Allah' offensives, and in anticipation of a fourth such offensive from 14 July he transferred Rawi's Guards Corps north from Maysan Province to Diyala Province, where it was inserted between I and II Corps. The corps had steadily gained experience since retaking the Faw Peninsula, and the combination of expertise and equipment made it the most formidable command on the Iran-Iraq frontline. Saddam was planning one last 'harvest' of Iranian military power to bring Iran to heal, and to buy time he refused to implement the cease-fire and demanded facetoface talks on all aspects of a peace agreement.

The new offensive, Operation Tawakkalna ala Allah-4, was the most ambitious and also the largest offensive launched by the Iraqi Army. It included four corps headquarters (I Special, II, III and Republican Guards) with 20 divisions, twice the strength of the one which crossed the border in September 1980, deployed on a front 170 kilometres long and 70 kilometres deep.[151] Units involved were to advance for up to 70 kilometres into Iran through mountainous terrain, in between peaks more than 2,000 metres high. The objective was to wreck the enemy ground forces and to take as many prisoners as possible to exchange for the thousands of Iraqi prisoners, while simultaneously regaining all lost Iraqi territory. Each corps was ordered to complete operations within 72 hours; with photographic reconnaissance and COMINT providing a detailed picture of the enemy forces and defences.

The Guards Corps was to take Sar-e Pol-e Zahab and Gilan-e Gharb but II Corps was to launch the main blow on a 120-kilometre front from north of Mandali to Mehran, taking the Sanuba Plateau, which dominates the Sumar Valley, and the Saif Saad Plateau within 72 hours. I Special Corps had a secondary role to secure the Mehran area but be ready to support its neighbours. The Southern Front's III Corps would also participate in the erosion of enemy strength.[152] Preparations began on 14 July with extensive aerial photography and scouting, and in addition to the arrival of the Guards, II Corps was reinforced by 10th Armoured Division, 7th and 8th Infantry Divisions from I Corps, and 5th Mechanized Division from IV Corps. Tawakkalna ala Allah-4 was scheduled to begin on 25 July 1988, but Y-Day was then brought forward to 22 July to pre-empt any diplomatic effort to end the war before Baghdad was ready.

Rawi, on the Iraqi left, had the Hammurabi and Medina Armoured Divisions, the Baghdad Infantry Division, and Nebuchadnezzar Mixed Division. Furthermore, he had two brigades of Tawalkalna ala Allah Armoured Division, 24 artillery battalions (432 guns and MLRS), a FROG battalion, 18 heavy mortar batteries (108 x 120mm tubes), and a combat engineering battalion. Baghdad, north of Qasr-e Shirin, was to take Sar-e Pol-e Zahab and raid the nearby headquarters of 81st Infantry Division IRIA, and also to strike its most forward supply bases to destroy heavy weapons and vehicles. Hammurabi and Medina would advance along the valleys on Baghdad's right. Meanwhile the Special Operations Division would capture Gilan-e-Gharb in a heliborne assault, and hold it until relieved by a mechanised brigade of 5th Mechanized Division, advancing from Mandali through Sumar, which would be handed

to the MeK. Nebuchadnezzar would be in reserve.

II Corps, under former Special Forces commander Major General Kamel Saji Aziz, was organized as detailed in Table 9. His units included 10th Armoured Division, 5th Mechanized Division, 16th, 21st, 22nd, and 28th Infantry Divisions, an armoured brigade from 17th Armoured Division, two independent armoured brigades, a commando brigade, 20 artillery battalions (with 360 guns and MLRS), 12 heavy mortar batteries (72 tubes), a FROG brigade, and five engineering battalions. It was to advance on six divisional fronts:

- 21st Infantry Division to take the Zayn al Qaws Plateau then advance upon Ghila e-Gharb and headquarters of 58th Infantry Division IRIA;
- 5th Mechanized Division, flanked by 16th Infantry Division, was to take the Sanuba Plateau then push on to Ghilan e-Gharb;
- 10th Armoured Division was to strike into the Sumar Valley to take both 88th Armoured Division IRIA's headquarters and WOHQ forward headquarters;
- 28th Infantry Division was to cover the right flank of 10th Armoured Division;
- 22nd Infantry Division was to take the Saif Saad Plateau and then 84th IRIA Division's headquarters during the night from 23 to 24 July, while
- The remainder of 22nd Infantry Division, supported by a brigade from 17th Armoured Division, a commando and a Special Forces brigade, would take the Meimak Heights.

I Special Corps would secure Mehran and from 30 June, it took over this sector from IV Corps; it was substantially reinforced from 14-18 July, and in addition to 1st, 2nd and 3rd Special Infantry Divisions it had one armoured brigade, one infantry and two commando brigades, 12 artillery battalions (216 guns), 3 heavy mortar batteries (18 tubes), and three engineering battalions. Its 2nd Special Infantry Division had already taken the Shahabi Plateau on 30 June and now it would occupy the mountains north of Mehran down to the Kunjan Dam and the mountains to the south down to Dehloran. There was the usual powerful air support with the 2nd and 4th IrAAC Air Wings providing 180 helicopters, while the IrAF deployed 125 aircraft in five CAS squadrons, a multi-role squadron with Mirage, and an air defence squadron, as well as electronic warfare and photo reconnaissance detachments.

This front was also largely an IRIA bailiwick under NFOHQ with five IRIA divisions (three armoured, two infantry) with 16 artillery battalions (200 guns/MLRS) and some smaller Pasdaran formations. In the Qasr e-Shirin/Sar-e Pol-e Zahab area was 81st Armoured Division, some Pasdaran brigades and six artillery battalions. In the Gilan-e Gharb area was 58th Infantry Division reinforced by 37th Independent Armoured and 55th Airborne Brigades, Sumar had 88th Armoured Division, at Sar Ney was 84th Infantry Division, and in Salehabad was 16th Armoured Division. The presence of two armoured divisions in mountainous terrain unsuitable for armour was an interesting commentary on Iran's strategic perspective and its growing shortage of resources.

The Last Attack

The attack began before dawn on 22 July 1988 as Iraqi engineers began clearing passages through minefields. The work was largely complete when the artillery preparation began at 06:25, paving the way for the infantry assault after 50 minutes. The combination of powerful artillery support, more than 1,000 tubes and MLRS, together with well-rehearsed tactics meant that most of the frontline positions were in Iraqi hands by 10:00 and their mechanised forces pushed into Iran as the temperature rose to 50°C with large amounts of water needed to prevent heat exhaustion.

In the Guards Corps the reinforced 'Baghdad' Division struck the Sisar Heights northeast of Sar-e Pol-e Zahab, and it was its armoured brigade which broke through the defences which were cleared by its infantry brigades. Its mechanised brigade took the pass leaving the commandos and armoured forces to follow the road to Sar-e Pol-e Zahab. Pausing only to refuel and refill ammunition lockers 'Baghdad' renewed its advance eastward the following day with its 9th Armoured Brigade taking an IRIA base and destroying all the equipment. 'Hammurabi' advanced along the Qasr-e Shirin to Sar-e Pol-e Zehab road, seizing both towns, and was then leapfrogged by 'Medina' which continued south on the route to Eman Hassan. Once Emam Hassan had been captured, 'Medina' turned southeast towards Ghilan e-Gharb where, on the evening of 23 July, part of 16th Special Forces Brigade of the Republican Guards Corps was landed by 100 helicopters behind the 81st Infantry Division's headquarters, which it soon captured with artillery and gunship support (the troops were flown up to 70 kilometres in the deepest Iraqi heliborne operation of the war). That evening they were relieved by the Guards Special Operations Division from the north, and the II Corps' 5th Mechanized Division from the south.

The II Corps fought a series of private divisional wars which are described from north to south, watched carefully not only by the corps commander but also Saddam. The reinforced 21st Infantry Division struck from Qasr-e Shirin to clear the Zayn al Qaws Plateau in three hours, then advanced upon Gilan-e Gharb which it also took after a short, sharp, fight. 5th Mechanized Division struck out north of Sumar to take Sanuba Plateau then pushed eastwards. The infantry overran the defences, then 20th Mechanized Brigade pushed deep into enemy territory to outflank the Sanuba Plateau from the south, isolating it by the afternoon to cause panic and confusion among the enemy. Behind it 26th Armoured Brigade advanced and quickly took Zarneh, while 16th Infantry Division mopped up the Sanuba Plateau. Meanwhile, 5th Mechanized Division pushed on to Gilan-e Gharb from the south through the night of 23/24 July and relieved the Guards in the town, whose isolated garrison now surrendered.

The 10th Armoured and 28th Infantry Divisions broke into the Sumar Valley outflanking enemy strongpoints to penetrate the defences, with many strong points isolated. In the early hours of 23 July the 10th also took 88th Division's headquarters near Sumar, and on the night 24/25 July took the NFOHQ forward command post. On its right 28th Infantry Division, which had returned from I Corps, crossed the Talkhab River and collected much booty including some Scud missiles.

The 22nd Infantry Division took the Saif Saad Plateau during the morning of 23 July, then advanced upon the village of Sar Ney where it overran 84th Division's headquarters on the night of 23/24 July. One of its brigades then advanced south to the village of Salehabad where it linked up with I Special Corps forces on 25 July. The 17th Armoured Division headquarters, with 22nd Division, commando and Special Forces brigades, had actually attacked first on the evening of 21/22 July to take the Warzin Plateau, easing its task the following day of isolating Sar Ney by taking the Meimak Heights.

To the south, following the 2nd Special Division's success in taking the Shehabi Plateau on 30 June, the I Special Corps attacked on the night of 19/20 July. The seasoned troops overran the enemy defences in the mountains east of Mehran aided by powerful artillery support, and on 24 July its commandos struck

the enemy defences in the Kunjan Dam sector opening the way for its armoured brigade. The brigade, with 2nd Special Division's commando battalion, pushed north from Mehran to attack Salehabad on 25 July with 50th Armoured Brigade (12th Armoured Division), and captured the 16th Armoured Division's headquarters after several hours of hard fighting. The corps then linked up with II Corps' 22nd Infantry Division. The corps' secondary operation was southeast of Mehran along the Iranian frontier road towards Dehloran, overcoming rugged terrain and numerous rivers with blown bridges, to complete their mission on 27 July. Sadly 2nd Special Forces Division's commander, Major General Salman Shuja Sultan, was killed in a plane crash.

Curiously, the largest Iraqi offensive in the war is largely ignored by most historians. Iranian casualties are unknown, although it is known that Major Generals Mostafa Pazhubandeh and Reza Nikkah were killed on 22 July. The Iraqi booty was reported to be 12,000 prisoners, 270 MBTs, 240 APC/ICVs, 250 guns (50 self-propelled) and 20 surface-to-surface missiles. This marked the end of Iraqi operations on the Central Front, but the last battle in this region would be de-facto an episode of the Iranian civil war.

The Odyssey of the NLA

The fuse was already lit by the Iranian success on the Faw Peninsula, Val Fajr-8, in early 1986. This raised French doubts about Saddam's ability to win the war and pay his massive debts for French equipment and led to a diplomatic rapprochement with Tehran. France, which had once offered Khomeinei sanctuary, was the natural home for Iran's exiled politicians, including former President Abol Hassan Bani-Sadr and his son-in-law, the leader of the Iranian Mujahideen e-Khalq (MeK), Massoud Rajavi. The latter were drawn from the Liberal/Left secularists who, with the elimination of enemies within the armed forces, posed the greatest internal threat to the Islamic Revolution.

Driven underground, the MeK hoped Bani-Sadr would rally the secularists, but these hopes were dashed when Khomeinei dismissed Bani-Sadr in in June 1981 (See Volume 1 p.48). The MeK then began a ferocious bombing campaign against the leaders, killing President Muhammad Ali Rajai and Prime Minister Muhhammad Javed Bahonar, but like all terror campaigns this rebounded, for it appalled traditional supporters such as the young middle class and skilled working class, who reluctantly supported the Islamic Revolution – for patriotic reasons – after the Iraqi invasion. In February 1982 the MeK's central committee were killed, and within months the organisation's military allies were destroyed when the Ghotbzadeh (or Qutbzadeh) Plot was uncovered. The survivors fled abroad to Paris and Baghdad, and by the end of 1982 the Iranian clerics felt confident that the threat had been contained and eased political repression, but remained wary of the threat resurfacing.[153]

Paris may have hoped a potential secular, pro-Western, opposition would return to Tehran and overthrow the government. The émigrés, however, spent more energy bickering among themselves, and by 1986 the French government had probably concluded that, as was noted: 'The ....Mujahedin was always better at publicity than at fighting'.[154]

Rajavi promoted the wife of a crony to the position of co-leader and then married her. Subsequently he fell out with both his wife and Bani-Sadr, established a personality cult, and – 'for ideological reasons' – then purged the movement of all his critics, which lead to additional desertions.[155] Another reason for dwindling émigré support was the closer relations between the MeK and Iraq, Rajarvi meeting Iraqi Foreign Minister Tariq Aziz in January 1983.

Iraqi armour (including T-62M MBTs), covered by a (US-made) Hughes MD.500 helicopter, on the advance in July 1988. (Albert Grandolini Collection)

A Mi-25 helicopter gunship of the IrAAF, returning from a combat sortie in support of Operation Tawakkalna ala Allah-4, in July 1988. (via Ali Tobchi)

Eventually, Paris decided it had backed the wrong horse and with numerous Iranian-sponsored kidnappings of its citizens abroad, as well as bombings within Metropolitan France, the new government of Jacques Chirac sought a rapprochement with Tehran amounting to appeasement. As part of this policy they expelled Iranian Mujahideen leader Masoud Rajarvi from his headquarters in Paris in June 1986, and following earlier contacts with Saddam, who would exploit the MeK, he now moved to Baghdad.

A year later he created a conventional army, the NLA (Artesh-e Azadibakhsh Melli Iran), whose baptism of fire was in the Northern Front on 3 July 1987, when a detachment struck in the Sar Dasht area east of Qalat Dizah to close a Kurdish supply route. The NLA took some peaks in a 15-hour battle, and the day saw several cross-border raids into western Azerbaijan, Ilam and Khuzistan Provinces. Similar operations continued through-out the year, 99 operations being claimed by the end of the year. They led Baghdad to conclude that the NLA would be best deployed on the Central Front. Its first operation was launched on 27 March 1988. Code-named Rising Sun, it saw a surprise attack by 12 'brigades' against 3rd Brigade of 77th Infantry Division IRIA, west of Shush, close to the Fakkeh-Dezful road. Rajavi claimed to have taken 1,000 square kilometres, and captured 500 prisoners and four MBTs.[156]

The success fed Rajavi's ambitions and, to strengthen his political hand, he opted to seize an Iranian town which would be a beacon for domestic discontent. Mehran was the most obvious objective and the NLA began preparations for Operation 'Chelcheragh' (chandelier) (Most accounts say this was Operation 'Forty Stars' but it was actually 'Chandelier'.) Ataii was aided by the staff of Iraq's II Corps, for Baghdad undoubtedly welcomed a diversion as it was about to launch Tawakkalna ala Allah-2 in the Hawaizah Marshes. While the MeK would later claim it struck independently, there is no doubt the NLA was supported by 17th Armoured Division and II Corps' artillery. This provided a heavy bombardment against

the defences of 11th Amir al-Momenin Infantry Division IRGC, supported by 2nd and 3rd Brigades of the IRIA's 16th Armoured Divison (some 20,000 troops).

The attack on 18 June was launched by 22 NLA 'brigades' (probably 11,000 men) but it was almost certainly the Iraqi troops who actually assaulted the defences and pushed back the defenders. The attackers beat off a major counter-attack on 21 June, to secure Mehran the following day, aided by 530 fixed and rotary wing sorties. The NLA claimed it suffered only 310 casualties, an indication that it actually took a secondary role, before extending its control to key bridges which it blew up, but after three days it withdrew across the border. A considerable amount of booty was acquired, the NLA claimed it was worth $2 billion, including 38 Chieftain MBTs, 30 guns (half of these self-propelled), and large numbers of Toyota trucks as well as 1,500 prisoners.[157]

Acutely aware that the war was now drawing to a close, the MeK pondered its options, and Rajavi decided to gamble on exploiting Iranian demoralisation by sending the NLA deep into Iran, to test popular support, in Operation 'Forougheh Javidan' (Eternal Fire). Once again II Corps provided assistance, moving the NLA northwards to its Sar-e Pol-e Zahab bridgehead, but with the possible exception of Special Forces, the Iraqi Army intended to sit on the sidelines, partly to ensure there were no obstacles to the planned ceasefire.

Saddam's attitude was ambiguous, for he was willing to support anyone who might undermine Iran's theocratic regime, but if it failed he had no intention of tying Iraq to a political corpse. He and the Iraqi Army leaders recognized that the NLA could never reach Tehran under its own power (or at least they said so to Rajawi, who would never listen) but, were still willing to provide artillery and air support, although the latter would suddenly cease when the NLA's fortunes turned (Comment by General Makki.). The MeK leadership talked of marching upon Tehran, a distance of 600 kilometres, but their initial objective was to establish a bridgehead around Qasr-e-Shirin, Sar-e-Pol-e-Zahab, Kerend, Islamabad and Kermanshah, establish a provisional government and encourage their supporters to rally.

The advance by 16 'brigades', with some 7,000 men and women supported by 35 EE-9 Cascaval wheeled reconnaissance vehicles, began at 15:30 on 25 July under NLA deputy commander Maryam Rajavi and Chief-of-Staff Mahmoud Atai'I, in five task forces under themselves, Deputy Chief-of-Staff Mehdi Bara'i, Ebrahim Zakeri, Mehdi Eftekhari and Mahmoud Mahdavi who found themselves facing Pasdaran and Basiji. The NLA drove eastward down the road from Qasr-e Shirin led by a fast-moving 'brigade' which took Kerend by 19:00, driving out the 127th Meghdad Brigade IRGC. The attackers now paused as reports flooded in of enemy troops assembling, and the NLA strengthened its positions by securing heights around the town on 27 July. However, its southern flank remained exposed and its supply line to Qasr-e Shirin was very narrow. The following day saw increasing Pasdaran attacks with air support, and COMINT indicated the enemy was trying to isolate the task force which withdrew across the border on the night of 28/29 July.[158]

Operation Mersad

The Iranians feared an NLA operation, and on 22 July 1988 President Khamenei warned 'that a group of hypocrites, two-faced and evil persons may appear in the country supported by foreign propaganda, who may try to break our national pride'.[159] Tehran might have believed that divine fortune ensured the regime's survival at this point. The Iraqi offensives had wrecked the IRIA and while the NFOHQ forward command post was reformed on 29 July it had only the remnants of the IRIA's 58th, 81st, 84th Divisions and 55th Airborne Brigade, which could offer only token resistance. But earlier in the month Tehran had decided to move its reserve of relatively fresh Pasdaran divisions from the Northern Front to prop up the battered Southern Front. Poor communications slowed the response. Nevertheless, by late July some 115,000 battle-hardened Pasdaran troops were flooding south and southeast, placing them across the NLA's planned line-of-advance. Other Pasdaran formations came up from the Central Front, as Tehran planned their annihilation in Operation 'Mersad' (Ambush) directed by Lieutenant General Sayyad Shirazi. This operation would use much of the IRIA's remaining armour while the IRIAA deployed 45 helicopters, including a dozen gunships, while three IRIAF CAS squadrons with F-5 Freedom Fighters were also deployed. The helicopters, three of which would be damaged, moved 3,360 troops and evacuated 388 wounded. Iranian air power claimed 29 APCs.

These troops were placed under Task Force Najaf-2, which first tried to stop another NLA column of five 'brigades' advancing from Kerend upon Eslamabad-e Gharb on 25 July, but the Najaf-2 garrison were driven out of Eslamabad by 22:00. Yet the three-'brigade' garrison quickly came under growing pressure, during the next three days, from the 5th Nasr, 17th Ali-ibn-Abu Taleb Infantry Divisions, and 43rd Imam Ali Engineer Division IRGC in the north. From the south the 8th Najaf Ashraf, 25th Karbala, 27th Mohammad Rasooallah, and 57th Abolfazl al-Abbas Divisions were reportedly attacking. By 27 July these had been joined by 71st Ruhollah Division and 155th Shohada Divisions, with 89th

A scene from the MEK/MKO's 'highway of death': following a series of fierce strikes by the IRIAF and the IRIAA, the road to Eslamabad was left clogged full of burned out tanks, vehicles and bodies of the NLA. (Albert Grandolini Collection)

Pasdaran of the 27th Rasoolallah Infantry Division IRGC during a break in fighting, in the Soleimaniyah area, in June 1988. (via N. S.)

An EE-9 Cascavel armoured car on advance into Iran in July 1988. (Albert Grandolini Collection)

A column of MT-LB APCs of the NLA, on the start of their advance into Iran. (Albert Grandolini Collection)

Moharram Artillery Brigade tightening the noose around the NLA, which was driven back across the border on the evening of 28 July.

Meanwhile, Eslamabad had barely fallen when the NLA pushed a 'brigade' forward towards Kermanshah. They were briefly held at the Chehar Zebar Pass by 33rd al-Mahdi Infantry Division, some 25 kilometres from Kermanshah, then pushed on only to be held by the newly arrived 31st Ashura and 32nd Ansar al-Hossein Divisions. The exposed NLA had no option but to withdraw during the morning of 28 July, pursued by the victorious defenders of the pass together with 9th Badr Division and 45th Javadol-A'emmeh Engineer Division.

Despite its claims, the NLA received little popular support in the areas which it 'liberated' because it was too closely associated with the Iraqis – making it abhorrent to patriotic Iranians. Rajavi's gamble had been a total failure; admitting the loss of 1,263 dead and missing, and 994 injured. The NLA also lost 72 AFVs, 21 122mm guns, and 612 other vehicles. Over 1,000 of its combatants were taken prisoner too, so that Rajavi had lost nearly half his army. Surprisingly, Tehran talked-up the NLA advance, claiming it threatened towns and cities far beyond its control. Whether or not this was panic, or a cynical ploy to encourage MeK supporters to expose themselves remains uncertain, but it did cause a wave of arrests inside Iran, and during the autumn between 1,000 and 5,000 were executed including many NLA prisoners.

Whatever happened inside Iran afterwards was a different story. Operation Mersad was the final act of the eight-years-long, bitter and bloody, Iran-Iraq War.

Peter Penev

Iran acquired 150 M48A5 Patton II MBTs, all equipped with the British-made 105mm guns, during the 1970s. Most of these went into the battle still painted in olive drab overall. However, many received disruptive camouflage patterns applied in medium green. This is a reconstruction prepared on basis of several photographs of different vehicles from the mid-1980s. (Artwork by Peter Penev)

Peter Penev

Each Iranian division included a reconnaissance regiment equipped with a company of British-made, Alvis FV.101 Scorpion light tanks – a total of 250 of which were acquired in the late 1970s. All of these were originally painted in light olive green overall. Scorpions proved reasonably effective during the first two years of the war, when some of more-skilled Iranian commanders used them to flank Iraqi armoured formations. One of the Iranian units equipped with Scorpions distinguished itself during the early fighting in the Ilam area, where it managed to temporarily stop the advance of the Iraqi 2nd Infantry Division. (Artwork by Peter Penev)

Peter Penev

Based on the chassis of the PT-76 light tank, the MT-LB was originally developed as the armoured variant of an artillery tractor (MT-L). In Iraqi service it was often armed with a ZU-23-2 anti-aircraft gun installed on the rear part of the hull. The Iranians captured about a dozen MT-LBs during the offensives of 1986-1987, and pressed them into service as APCs. Most were painted in dark sand overall, though some had a disruptive camouflage pattern in green, applied in very different forms. (Artwork by Peter Penev)

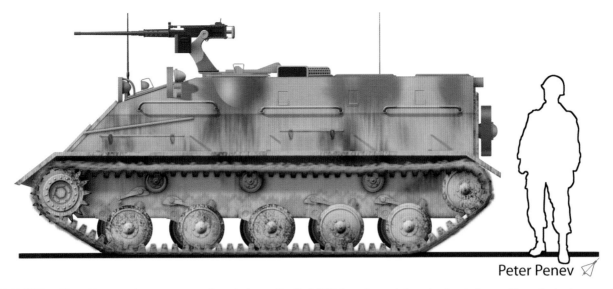

The OT M-60 (OT = oklopni transporter, or armoured carrier) was the first APC to enter serial production in former Yugoslavia. Iraq purchased 190 slightly improved M-60Ps in the mid-1980s, but very little is known about their service. Gauging from the few available photographs, all were painted in the standardised Iraqi Army camouflage pattern consisting of yellow sand and blue green, and have retained their US-made, 12.7mm Browning M2 machine gun as primary armament. (Artwork by Peter Penev)

The BRDM-2 amphibious scout car was the primary reconnaissance vehicle of Iraqi mechanised formations. The vehicle proved highly popular for its easy maintenance and reliability. This example shows how most of Iraqi BRDM-2s appeared early during the war, painted in the standardised Iraqi Army camouflage pattern of yellow sand and blue green. (Artwork by Peter Penev)

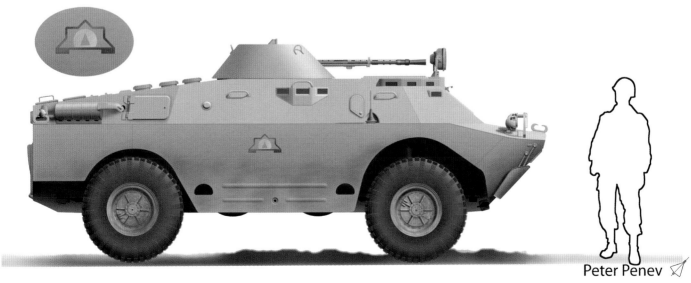

Later during the war with Iran, most Iraqi BRDM-2s were painted in yellow sand only – a colour that rapidly bleached into different shades of grey-sand. Many received tactical unit insignia of their parent formations – one example of which is illustrated in the inset. (Artwork by Peter Penev)

Peter Penev

The 2S1 Gvozdika self-propelled howitzer made a relatively late appearance in the Iran-Iraq War. While based on the extended chassis of the MT-LB carrier, they were equipped with a modified variant of the 122mm 2A18 towed howitzer. Gvozdikas became the primary equipment of two batteries in each artillery battalion of every armoured division as of 1987. All the examples known to have been operated by the Iraqis as of that time were painted in yellow-sand overall, and seem to have worn no special insignia. (Artwork by Peter Penev)

Peter Penev

The Iranians captured about a dozen 2S1s in 1986 and 1987, and the IRGC pressed them in service – usually after enhancing their camouflage through addition of a disruptive pattern in green. This is a reconstruction of a Gvozdika operated by the IRGC in 1988. (Artwork by Peter Penev)

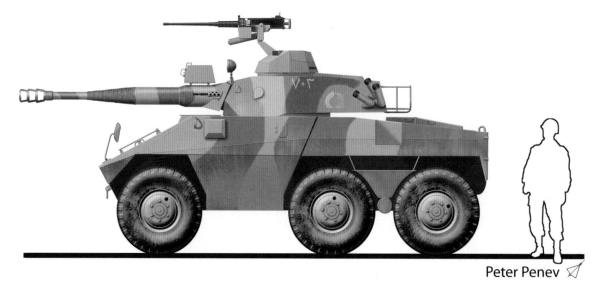

Peter Penev

The EE-9 Cascavel (Portuguese for 'Rattlesnake') is a six-wheeled armoured car of Brazilian origin, 364 of which were acquired by Iraq in the 1980s. At least a company worth of EE-9s was donated to the NLA, and deployed during its advance into Iran in July 1988. Atop the sand as primary colour, some received disruptive camouflage patterns in light green, and others in dark green. Most NLA vehicles had the crest of the MEK/MKO applied – either on the sides of the forward fuselage, or on the turret side. (Artwork by Peter Penev)

The M107 self-propelled howitzer was based on the chassis of the M578 light recovery vehicle. The lightly protected body (the armour was only 13mm thick), carried the 175mm cannon, installed on the rear of the vehicle without an armoured encasing – in turn offering more space for movement of the crew. The Iranians acquired only 38 M107s (and 38 similar M110s, armed with a 203mm howitzer) in the 1970s, but these were in much demand because they outranged most artillery pieces in Iraqi service. As far as is known, most went into battle still painted in olive drab overall, over which disruptive patterns in sand (as shown here), or other shades of green, were applied. (Artwork by Peter Penev)

With Iran acquiring no fewer than 430 self-propelled artillery pieces of this type, the M109A1s were the most important element of artillery groups of its army. Its primary armament consisted of the 155mm M185 howitzer. All vehicles were originally painted in light olive green overall. Never refreshed during the war with Iraq, their colour frequently dilapidated into various shades of grey-green and sand. (Artwork by Peter Penev)

The Pilatus PC-7 was a two-seat basic trainer aircraft, sold by Switzerland to both Iran and Iraq – starting in 1983. The Iraqi Army Aviation Corps was quick in adapting some of its 52 PC-7s for COIN purposes. The first unit equipped with the type became operational in 1984 and was deployed to fight Kurdish insurgents in the north of the country. It had all of its aircraft camouflaged as shown on this example (serial number 5024, c/n 170/9043). Colours used seem to have been of French origin, and included Brun Café (similar to BS381C/388 Beige), Brun Noisette (similar to BS381C/350 Dark Earth) and Gris Vert Fonce (similar BS381C/641 Dark Green) on top surfaces and sides. Undersurfaces were probably painted in a colour similar to Celomer 1625 Gris Bleu Moyen Clar (light blue-grey). The second IrAAC's unit of PC-7s was operational by 1986, by when PC-7s became frequent sights over the northern and central battlefields of the Iran-Iraq War. Their usual armament consisted of FN ETNA TMP-5 twin 7.62mm machine-gun pods and Matra F2 pods for six 68mm SNEB unguided rockets. (Artwork by Tom Cooper)

While playing a prominent role on the southern battlefield early during the war, most of IrAAC's SA.342 Gazelles were re-deployed towards the north later during the conflict. With anti-armour warfare being of lesser importance in these areas, they were frequently armed with 20mm GIAT M621 cannon (always installed on the right side of the helicopter only), and Brandt 68x12 or 68x22 launchers for 68mm SNEB unguided rockets. Some examples had improved exhaust pipes, illustrated in the inset, to decrease their exposure to infra-red homing MANPADs. (Artwork by Tom Cooper)

With southern battlefields proving too dangerous for them, most of about 50 SE.316C Alouette IIIs Iraq acquired in the 1970s served on the northern and central battlefields, where their significant 'hot and high' capabilities were of advantage. The type was equipped with the APX-Bézu 260 gyro-stabilised sight, which enabled the deployment of AS.12 ATGMs. Many Iraqi Alouette IIIs have received improved sand filters installed on their engine intakes during the second half of the 1980s. (Artwork by Tom Cooper)

In addition to the well-known Bell 214A Esfahan, no less than 335 of which were purchased by Iran in the 1970s in several major variants, the IRIAA also deployed about 70 Agusta-Bell AB.205A utility helicopters (essentially an export variant of the UH-1H Huey). Consisting of colours named earth yellow and field drab, the camouflage on their top surfaces and sides was slightly lighter than that on Esfahans, and they usually had the top side of their noses painted in black. While serials (in range 6-4300 upwards) were applied in black on the fin, most have received full service titles – in English and in Farsi – on cabin doors. (Artwork by Tom Cooper)

During the 1970s, the Iranian Army closely followed the helicopter-related developments and thinking of the US Army. When, based on experiences from Vietnam, the Americans decided to develop hunter-killer teams consisting of light scout helicopters and dedicated armoured attack helicopters, the Iranian army aviation followed in fashion. One of the results was the acquisition of 214 Bell 206s, the majority of which entered service with the army and were camouflaged as shown here, in dark sand and dark earth on top surfaces and sides, and light grey on undersurfaces. In addition to use as scouts, they were primarily deployed for utility purposes. The insets show an interim variant of the IRIAA's crest (applied on many of its Bell 206s and AH-1Js during the second half of the 1980s and later on), and the service title of the IRIAA in Farsi (more commonly known as 'Havaniruz'). (Artwork by Tom Cooper)

Although their numbers frequently dwindled to fewer than 50 operational examples due to combat attrition, incidents, and requirements of periodic maintenance, IRIAA's AH-1Js remained the most important means of close air support for army and IRGC troops throughout the war with Iraq. While still retaining their camouflage pattern in dark yellow-sand and dark earth over, and pale grey under, most began receiving standardised service titles: 'IRIAA' was usually retained on the boom, while the Farsi-version was applied below the pilot's (rear) cockpit, together with the new crest of the Havaniruz. Principal armament of AH-1Js consisted of the 20mm M197 gun and M260 (17 tubes, illustrated here) and M261 (7 tubes) launchers for 3.75in (68mm) unguided rockets. Frequent clashes with Iraqi helicopters and fighter-bombers led to some experimentation with installation of AIM-9J Sidewinder missiles, on adapters and rails illustrated on the inset. (Artwork by Tom Cooper)

Out of 202 AH-1J Cobras acquired by Iran in the 1970s, 65 were modified through the addition of M65 TOW sights and thus compatible with BGM-71 TOW ATGMs. They became the primary 'killers' of Iraqi armour during the war of 1980-1988. Despite frequent shortages of TOWs (mostly caused by problems related to the Iranian logistics, rather than true lack of rounds), carriage of eight rounds remained standard for most of that conflict. In addition to its standard camouflage pattern, this Cobra is shown wearing an 'interim' variant of service title – applied in white, in larger letters than usually, underneath the pilot's (rear) cockpit. Curiously, this example served for most of the war without the usual fin flash. (Artwork by Tom Cooper)

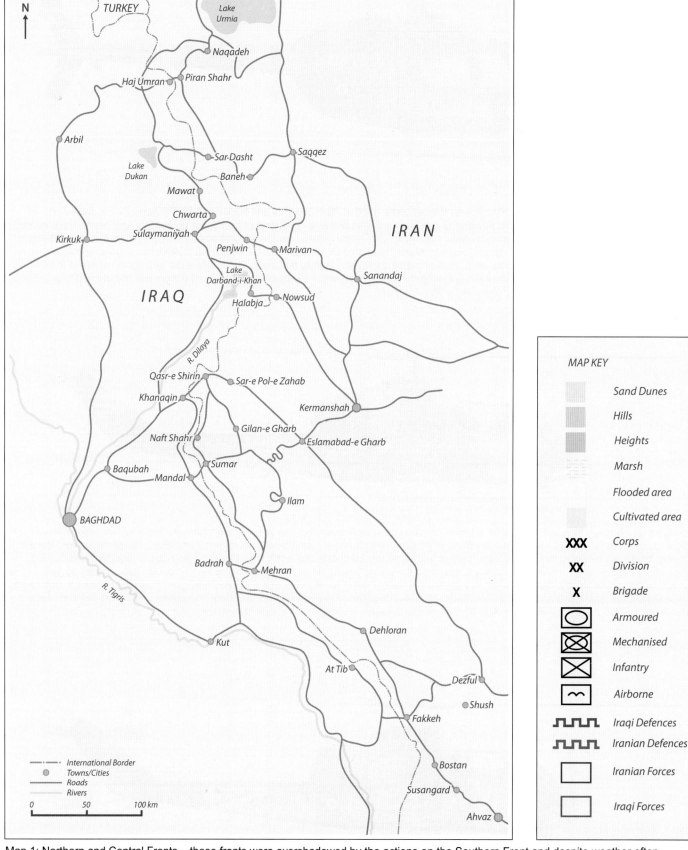

Map 1: Northern and Central Fronts – these fronts were overshadowed by the actions on the Southern Front and despite weather often reducing the campaigning season, they saw an astonishing diversity of operations. These included mechanised and mountain warfare as well as special operations against a background of the Kurdish insurgency with both Iran and Iraq conducting counter-insurgency operations.

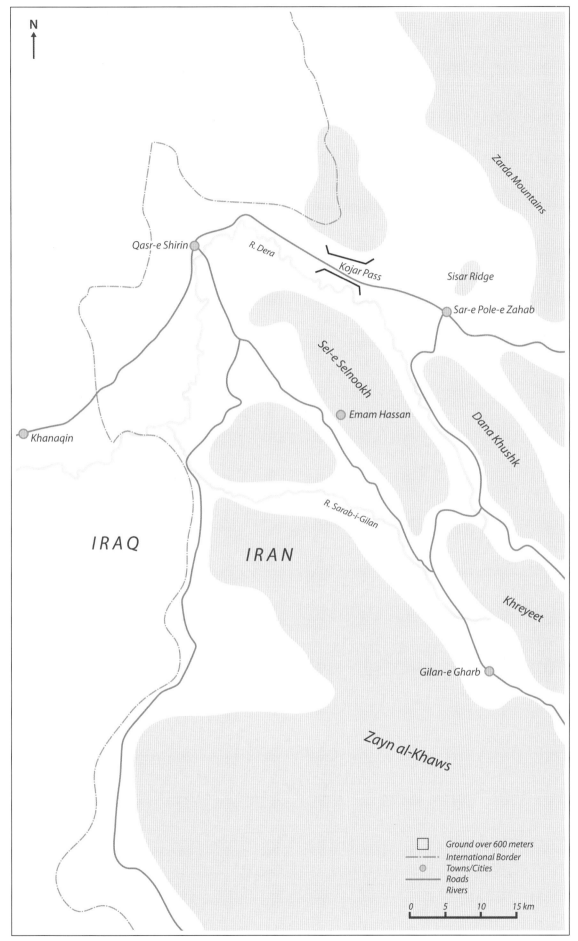

Map 2: The Qasr-e-Shirin Sector – this sector of mountains, split by river valleys, illustrated the swinging pendulum of fortunes. Territory won by the Iraqi invasion of 1980 was largely eroded by Iranian attacks within a couple of years but in 1988 it would become the jump-off point for the disastrous incursion by Iranian emigrés.

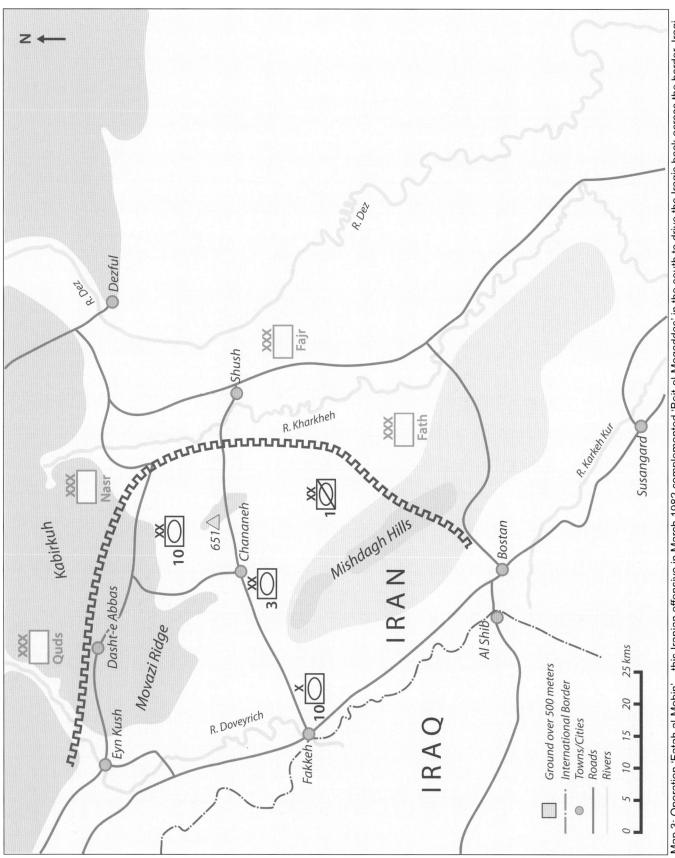

Map 3: Operation 'Fatah al-Mobin' – this Iranian offensive in March 1982 complemented 'Beit-ol-Mogaddas' in the south to drive the Iraqis back across the border. Iraqi forces facing strong pressure along the whole defensive arc were undermined by weak leadership which caused the defence to collapse leading to a chaotic retreat.

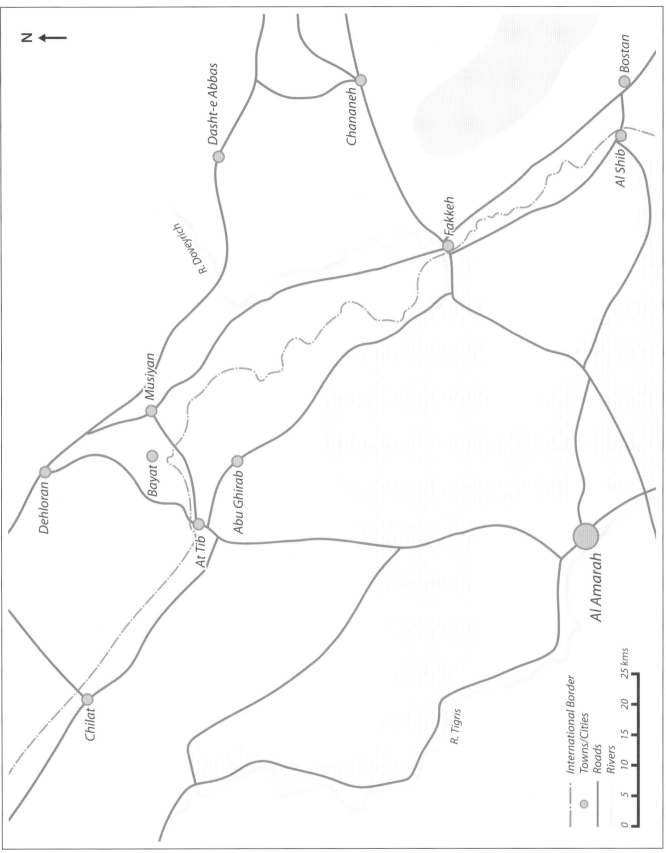

Map 4: Southern Central Front 1982-1987 – this was an area of largely open terrain with low heights making it suitable for mechanised operations. It was Iraqi superiority in armour, artillery and air power which helped to contain the numerous threats although they did gain some territory. This would be lost when Baghdad launched its own offensive in 1988.

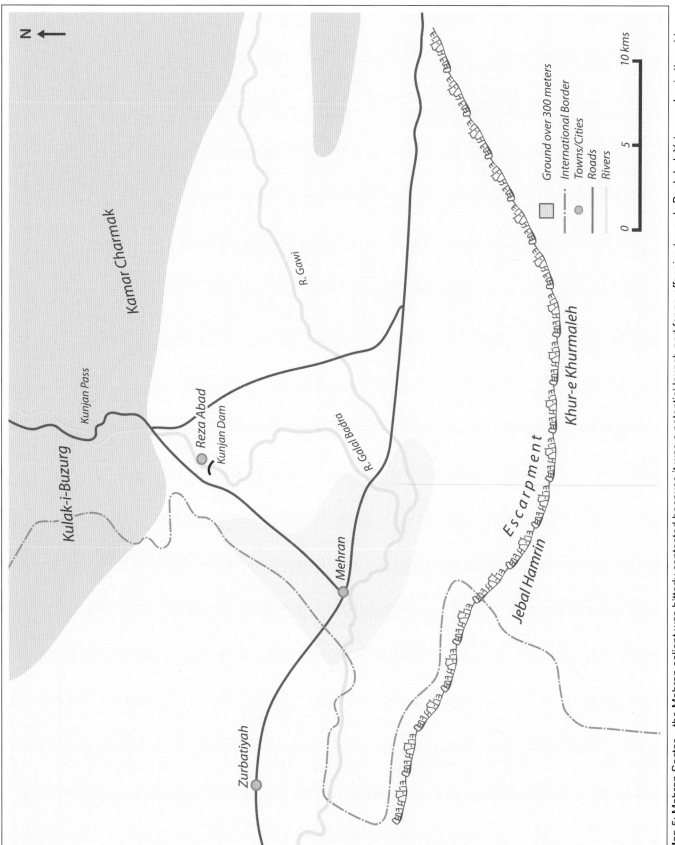

Map 5: Mehran Sector – the Mehran salient was bitterly contested because it was a potential launch pad for an offensive towards Baghdad. Yet every Iraqi attempt to hold the town was thwarted because they were exposed to Iranian infantry able to exploit the rough terrain surrounding it which neutralised Iraq's superior fire power.

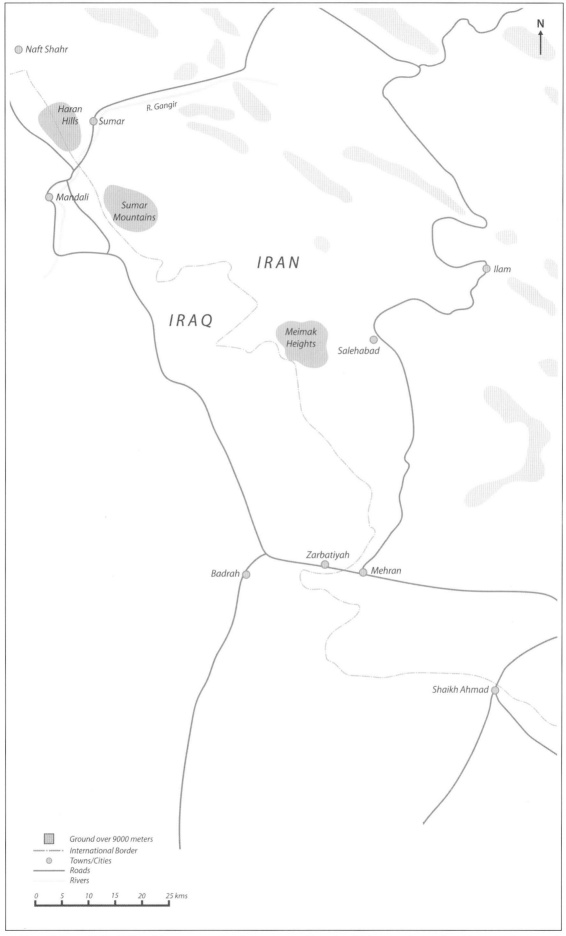

Map 6: Northern Central Front 1982-1987 – this was an area of more rugged terrain which severely restricted large scale operations. Most of the offensives in this sector tended to be to gain tactically useful high ground in regions such as the Meimak Heights, the Haran Hills and Sumar Mountains.

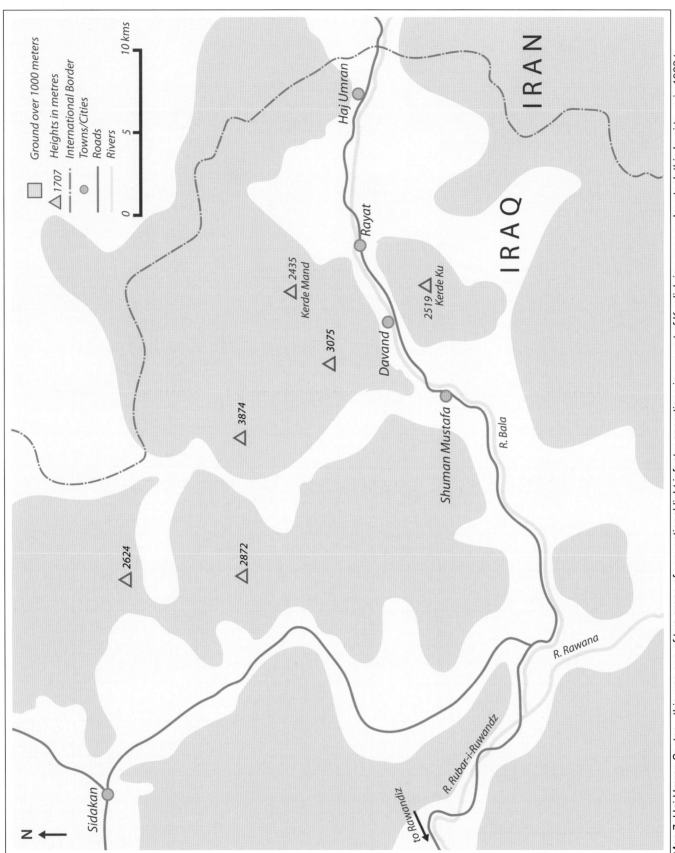

Map 7: Haj Umran Sector – this was one of two areas of conventional light infantry operations in support of Kurdish insurgency. Iran took this Iraqi town in 1982 to complete the defeat of the KDPI rebellion within its own borders and then attempted to drive supply corridors westward to Kurdish sanctuaries. While territory was gained the effort ultimately failed and in response to Iraqi offensives to the south it was abandoned in the summer of 1988.

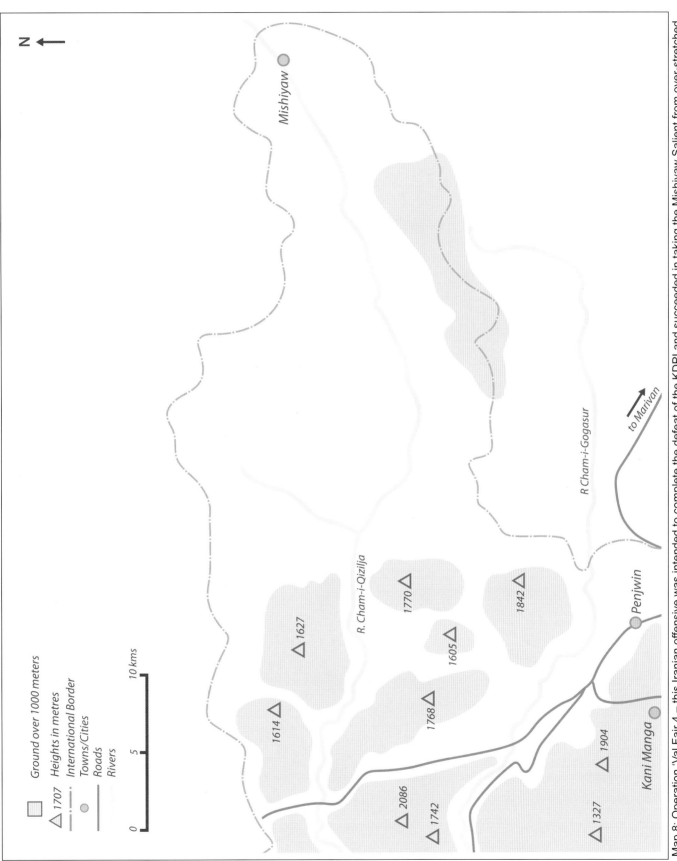

Map 8: Operation 'Val Fajr 4 – this Iranian offensive was intended to complete the defeat of the KDPI and succeeded in taking the Mishiyaw Salient from over-stretched defenders. Iraqi reinforcements succeeded in preventing any exploitation of this success which did help to stimulate a new Kurdish uprising in Iraq.

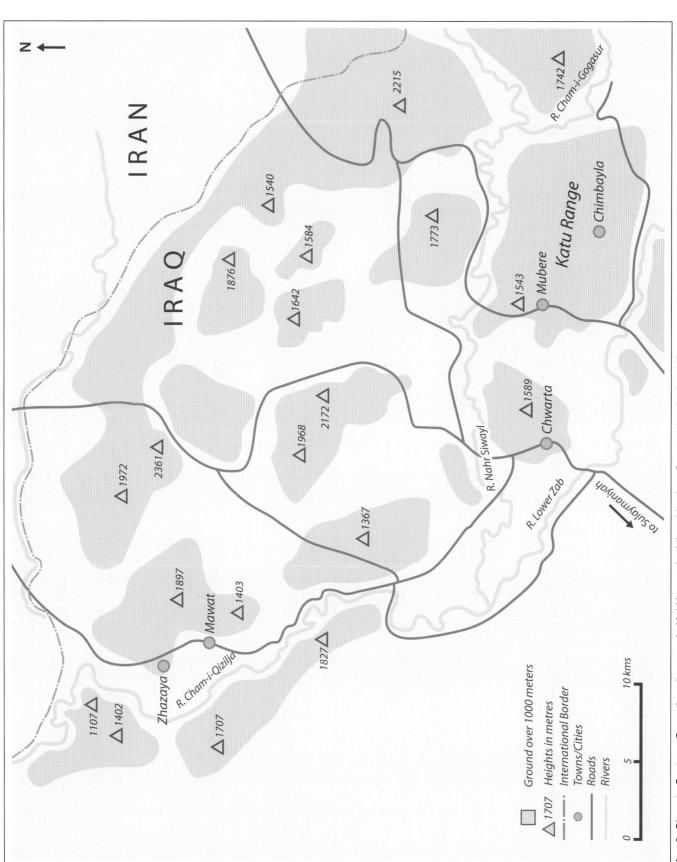

Map 9: Chwarta Sector – Operations here, as in Haj Umran, had the objective of supporting the Iraqi Kurds by opening supply corridors to their sanctuaries. Here too numerous Iranian offensives succeeded in pushing their line westward but ultimately they never established a secure corridor.

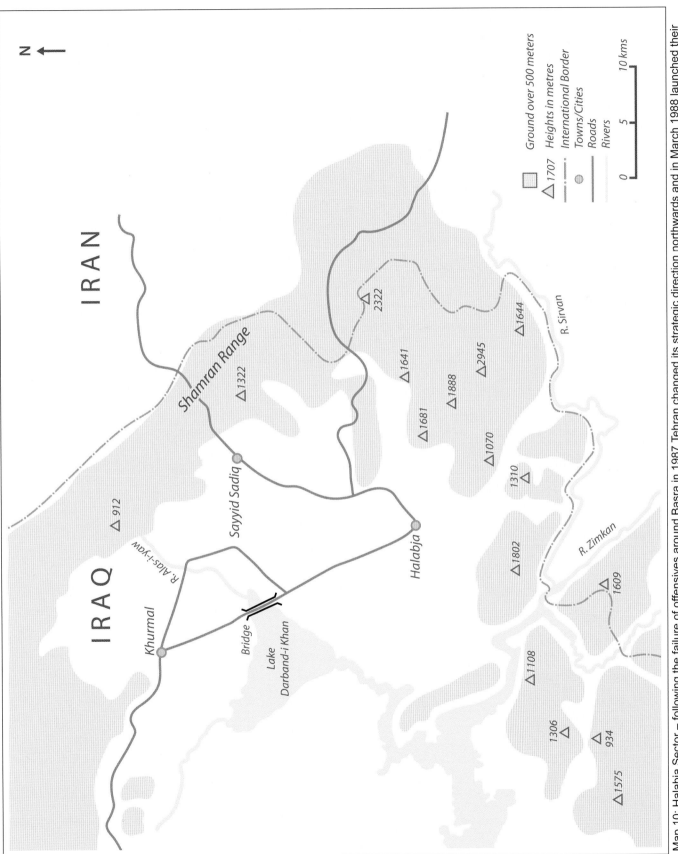

Map 10: Halabja Sector – following the failure of offensives around Basra in 1987 Tehran changed its strategic direction northwards and in March 1988 launched their largest operation in this theatre, 'Val Fajr 10' to drive a corridor to the nearest Kurdish sanctuary. The defence initially collapsed but quickly recovered to thwart the Iranian objective aided by the extensive use of chemical weapons, notably at the town of Halabja.

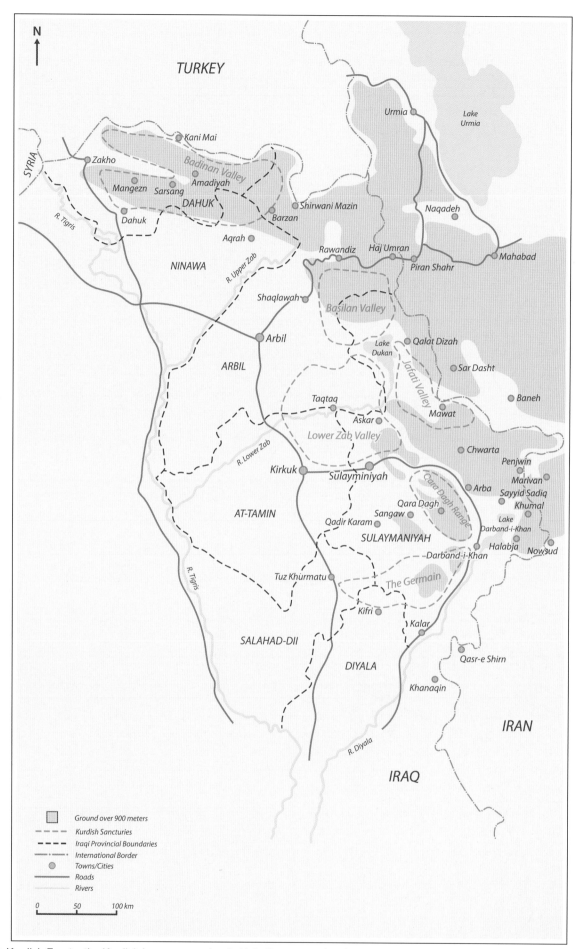

Map 11: The Kurdish Front – the Kurdish insurgency extended into three countries; Iraq, Iran and Turkey and the interplay of these struggles was reflected in operations within Iraq. Despite factionalism the Kurds had some success and controlled considerable territory by 1987 with several sanctuaries which could be destroyed only through the use of powerful forces. In 1988 this was what the Iraqis succeeded in doing with the 'Anfal' offensives.

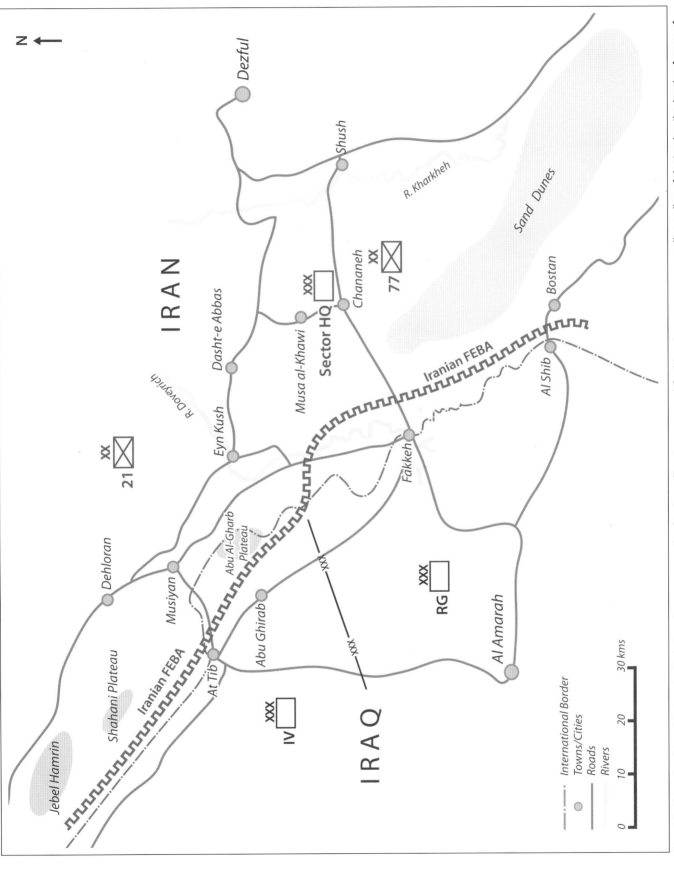

Map 12: Operation 'Tawakkalna ala Allah 3' – Successes on the Southern Front encouraged Saddam to pursue a war-ending policy of destroying the Iranian forces of which 'Tawakkalna ala Allah 3' on the southern Central Front was the fourth phase. Launched on July 12 it smashed the defenders to take up to 7,000 prisoners and much equipment and led to Tehran's pledge to withdraw from Haj Umran.

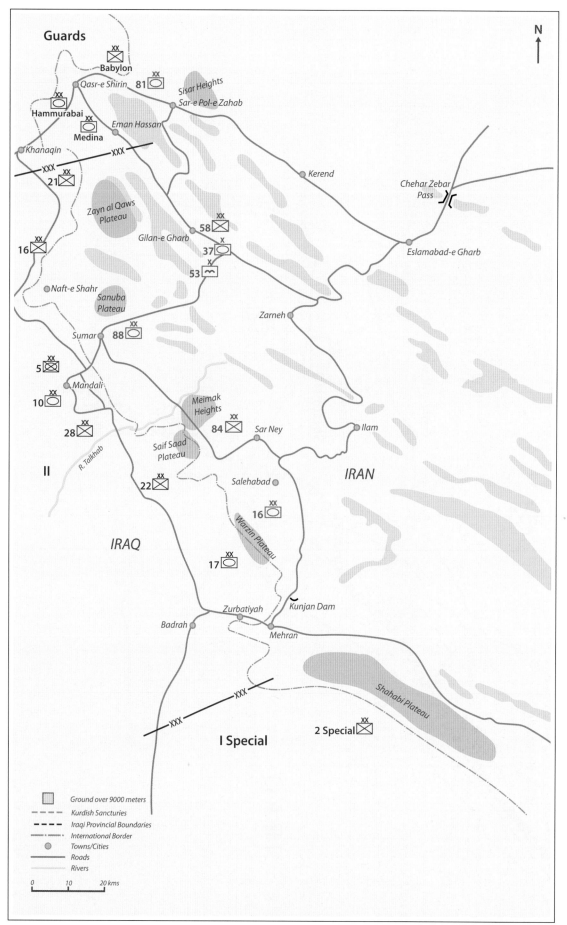

Map 13: Operations 'Tawakkalna ala Allah 4' and 'Eternal Fire' – the last and biggest offensive of the war 'Tawakkalna ala Allah 4' was launched on July 22 on a 120 kilometre front and was another success which reportedly took 12,000 prisoners and helped to force Iran to accept an armistice. In the north it also established jump-off points for the Iranian emigrés' disastrous 'Eternal Fire' offensive.

BIBLIOGRAPHY

Books

Buchan, James, *Days of God: The revolution in Iran and its consequences* (London: John Murray, 2013).

Bulloch, John and Harvey Morris, *The Gulf War: Origin, History and Consequences of Islam at War* (London: Methuen Publishers, 1989).

Connell, Michael, *Iranian Operational Decision Making: Case Studies from the Iran-Iraq War* (Alexandria VA: CNA Analysis & Solutions, 2013) (Cached copy of (http//www) dtic.mil/dtic/tr/fulltext/u2/a585872.pdf)

Cooper, Tom & Farzad Bishop, *Iran-Iraq War in the Air 1980-1988* (Atglen PA: Schiffer Military History, 2000).

Cordesman, Anthony H., *The IranIraq War and Western Security 19841987* (RUSI Military Power Series), (London: Jane's Publishing Company Ltd, 1987).

Cordsman, Anthony H. & Abraham R. Wagner, *The Lessons of Modern War: Volume IIThe IranIraq War* (Boulder CO/San Francisco CA: Westview Press and London: Mansell Publishing Ltd,1990).

Farrokh, Dr Kaveh, *Iran at War 1500-1980* (Oxford: Osprey Publishing, 2011).

Hiro, Dilip, *The Longest War: The IranIraq Military Conflict* (London: Paladin Grafton Books, 1989).

Khazraji, General (General Staff) Nizar Abdul Karim Faisal Al, *Al Harb Al Iraqiya- Al Iraniya) 1980-1988 Muthakerat Muqatel (The Iraq-Iran War1980-1988. Memoirs of a Fighter)* (Doha, Qatar: Arab Centre for Research & Policy Studies, 2014).

Khoury, Dina Rizk, *Iraq in Wartime: Soldiering, Martyrdom and Remembrance* (Cambridge: Cambridge University Press, 2013).

Makki Khamas (Makki) General Aladdin Hussein, *Maarik Al Tahrir Al Kubra Al Iraqiya 1988 (The Great Iraqi Battles of Liberation 1988)* (Amman, Jordan: Academiuoon Publishing Company, 2014).

Malovany, Colonel Pesach, *Wars of Modern Babylon* (Lexington KY: The University Press of Kentucky, 2017).

Al-Marashi, Ibrahim & Sammy Salama, *Iraq's Armed Forces: An analytical history* (London: Routledge, 2009).

Middle East Watch, *Genocide in Iraq: The Anfal Campaign Against the Kurds* (Washington: Human Rights Watch, 1993). From Genocide in Iraq web site.

Murray, Williamson and Kevin M. Woods, *The Iran-Iraq War: A Military and Strategic History* (Cambridge: Cambridge University Press, 2014).

Nixon, John, *Debriefing the President: The Interrogation of Saddam Hussein* (London: Transworld Publishers, Corgi Edition, 2017).

O'Ballance, Edgar, *The Gulf War* (London: Brassey's Defence Publishers, 1988).

Pelletiere, Stephen C., *The Iran-Iraq War: Chaos in a Vacuum* (Westport CT and London: Praeger, 1992).

Pelletiere, Stephen C. & Douglas V. Johnson, Leif R. Rosenberg, *Iraq Power and U.S. Security in the Middle East (*Carlisle Barracks, PA, Strategic Studies Institute, US Army War College, 1990)

Pollack, Kenneth M., *Arabs at War. Military effectiveness 1948-1991* (Lincoln NE & London: University of Nebraska Press, 2002).

Razoux, Pierre (translated by Nicholas Elliott), *The Iran-Iraq War* (London: The Belnap Press of Harvard University Press, 2015).

Taghvaee, Babak, *Desert Warriors: Iranian Army Aviation at War* (Solihull: Helion & Company, 2016.)

Ward, Steven R., *Immortal: A military history of Iran and its armed forces* (Washington DC: Georgetown University Press, 2009).

Woods, Kevin M. (With Williamson Murray & Thomas Holaday with Mounir Elkhamri), *Project 1946* (Alexandria VA: Virginia Institute for Defense Analyses, 2008).

Articles, Essays, Monographs, Papers, Reports, Theses

Banks, Tony, 'The changing war for Kurdistan', *Jane's Defence Weekly* 12 August 1989 p.249.

Colonel Eccles, R.G. (British Defence Attaché, Iraq) Review of the Iraq military situation August 1983-April 1986, April 27, 1986. These were kindly provided by the British Foreign Office under the Freedom of Information Act.

Grau, Lieutenant Colonel Lester W. and Lieutenant Jason Failvene, 'Mountain Combat: Hard to move, hard to shoot, even harder to communicate,' *Journal of Military Studies* September 2008.

Griffin, Lieutenant Colonel Gary B., 'The Iraqi Way of War: An operational assessment', School of Advanced Military Studies, United States Army Command and General Staff College, Fort Leavenworth, Kansas, 1990.

Lortz, Michael G. 'Willing to Face Death: A history of Kurdish Military Forces. The Peshmerga-From the Ottoman Empire to Present Day Iraq' (Electronic thesis from Florida State University 28 October 2005. Web site 'Willing to Face Death' citeseerx.ist.psu.edu/viewdoc/download?doc=10.1.1.661.6369&rep=rep)

O'Ballance, Colonel Edgar, 'Iran vs Iraq: Quantity vs Quality?' *Defence Attaché* No 1/1987, pp.25-31.

No author, *Jane's Defence Weekly*:

'Mujahideen strength growing in Iran', 28 December 1986.

'Kurdish villages razed in punitive Iraqi campaign', 10 October 1987.

'Kirkuk oilfield raid-damage disputed', 18 October 1987.

'NLA and the struggle against Tehran', 20 February 1988.

'Iraq in successful attack on occupied territory', 2 July 1988.

'Iraq's southern successes', 23 July 1988.

No author, *NLA Quarterly*:

'Operation 'Shining Sun', Spring 1988.

'Special Report', Autumn 1988.

'Disarming Khomeinei, Special Report', Autumn 1988.

'NLA Chief of Staff Describes Operation 'Shining Sun'', Spring 1988.

Scott, Aziz, 'PKK opens second front', *International Defense Review* 7/1991 pp.702-703.

Documents

CIA:

RDP90T00784R000100300010-1 British Chieftain Tank. Leningrad Tank Testing Area.

Conflict Record Research Center (CRRC):

SH-AFGC-D-000-686: Orders of the President and Commander-in-Chief of the Armed Forces February-December 1984.

SH-GMID-D-000-301 Reports from General Directorate of Military Intelligence regarding the Iraq and Iran War 1982-1987.

SH-GMID-D-000-337 Reports by the General Military Intelligence Directorate regarding movements of Iranian Divisions and current military operations on the border. 1988

SH-GMD-D-000-530 General Military Intelligence Directorate (GMID) Correspondence Regarding Reports on the Movements of Troops during the Iran-Iraq War. Apr 1988

SH-MISC-D-001-3740 Report on the Al-Sulaymaniyah Security Governate from 1985-1988 including An-Anfal

SH-PDWN-D-000-730: Transcript of an Armed Forces General Command meeting regarding the Iran-Iraq War, al-Fao, and military and diplomatic aspects of the war. May 26, 1988.

SH-SHTP-D-000-538: Transcript of a Meeting between Saddam and his Commanding Officers at the Armed Forces General Command Regarding the Iraq-Iran War. June 27 1988.

SH-SHTP-A-000-788 Saddam Discussing the Iraqi Stance Toward respecting International Law. Circa June-July 1988.

SH-SHTP-A-001-045. Saddam and High Ranking Officers Discussing Plans to Attack Kurdish 'Saboteurs' in Northern Iraq and the Possibiity of Using Special Ammunition (Weapons). Undated but circa 1985).

Defense Intelligence Agency:

DDB-1100-342-86: Ground Forces Intelligence Study-Iran (May 1986).

DDB-1100-343-85: Ground Forces Intelligence Study: Iraq (November 1985).

DDB-2680-103-88 Part II: Military Intelligence Summary: Volume III, Part II Middle East and North Africa (Persian Gulf) (Cut-off date 1 July 1987).

US Army Intelligence and Security Command:

Untitled and undated history of Iran-Iraq War from September 1980 to the spring of 1983.

Released under NGIA FOIA request NGA #20130255F and US Army Intelligence and Security Command request FOIA#2456F-12 on November 19, 2013. Declassified March 19, 2013.

Websites

Imposed War web site (www) sajed.ir or (http) English. tebyan,net.

(www) Ironsides8m.com/army/ir.htm~army

(www) iran-e-azad.org/English/nla/etl.html.

Genocide in Iraq. hrw.org/reports/1993/iraqanfal/ANFAL.htm

Anfal: The Iraqi State's Genocide against the Kurds, The Center of Halabja against Anfalization and genocide of the Kurds (CHAK), February 2007 www.wadinet.de/news/dokus/ Anfal_CHAK.pdf

NOTES

1   See Vol.1, p.4 & Lortz thesis, pp. 48-51.
2   Hiro, *The Longest War*, p. 35 (hereafter Hiro).
3   Murray & Woods, p. 332.
4   Patrick Bishop, 'The real Iraq menace now the war is over', *Daily Telegraph*, 13 September 1988.
5   Mahabad had been the heart of the Kurdish uprising and the emerging Kurdish autonomous republic established with support from the Union of Soviet Socialist Republics (USSR, also 'Soviet Union'), in December 1945. This was crushed by the Iranians within a year. It was during this period that the expression 'Peshmerga' became something like 'official'. See Lortz thesis, pp. 26-30 (hereafter Lortz).
6   For Kurdish operations in Iran in 1979-1980, see Lessons, pp. 26-27 & O'Ballance, pp. 132-133.
7   See Volume 1 for full backgrounds of the Iraqi decision to invade Iran.
8   Farrokh, *Iran at War*, p. 351 (hereafter Farrokh) & Malovany, *Wars of Modern Babylon*, pp. 124 & 141-142 (hereafter Malovany).
9   US Army Intelligence and Security Command history, p. 4.9 (hereafter AISC).
10 Farrokh, p.349 & Ward, *Immortal*, p.247 (hereafter Ward).
11 For air support, see Cooper & Bishop, *Iran-Iraq War in the Air*, pp. 83, 85-86, 89, 96-97 (hereafter Cooper & Bishop) & Farrokh, p. 352.
12 Cooper & Bishop, pp. 67-68, 96; Farrokh, pp.351-352; Hiro, pp.40-41; Cordesman & Wagner, *The Lessons of Modern War*, p.85 (Hereafter Lessons); Malovany, pp. 116-121; Murray & Woods, *The Iran-Iraq War*, pp.111-113 (herafter Murray & Woods); O'Ballance, *The Gulf War*, pp. 33 & 35 (hereafter O'Ballance); AISC, pp. 4-11; Conflict Record and Resource Center (CRRC) SH-SHTP-D-000-847. Note that some sources erroneously credit 7th Mountain Division with taking Qasr-e Shirin.
13 Cross-examination of different reports shows the 30th Armoured Brigade lost a third of its MBTs destroyed or damaged, and being left with a weak mechanized infantry battalion and its organic special forces battalion only.
14 Murray & Woods, p. 116.
15 CRRC SH-PDWN-D-001-021.
16 Cooper & Bishop, pp. 101-102.
17 O'Ballance, p. 35; Hiro p.41.
18 For operations around Mehran see Farrokh, p. 352; Hiro, p. 41; Lessons, pp. 8587; Malovany, pp. 121-122; Murray & Woods, p. 115; O'Ballance, pp. 35-36; AISC, pp. 4-13; CRRC SH-MISC-D-000-827, SH-PDWN-D-001-021 and SH-SHTP-D-000-847.
19 CRRC SH-PDWN-D-001-021

20 Information on commanding Iraqi officers from General Makki. Reports that the 4th and 7th Infantry Divisions advanced on Fakkeh and Bostan are now known to be inaccurate.
21 AISC pp. 4-13 & 4-19.
22 See Volume 1 for details.
23 Murray & Woods, pp. 147-148.
24 Cooper & Bishop, p. 112; Hiro, p.49; Lessons, p.96; Malovany, p. 154; O'Ballance, pp. 4142. Notable is that many Iranian martyrs of the war with Iraq were posthumously advanced at least one, sometimes two ranks. Because there is no certainty in each case, only their last known ranks are mentioned – which are likely to be higher than while they were still alive.
25 Hiro, p.49; Malovany, p.174; O'Ballance, pp. 4142, 133-134.
26 Malovany, pp. 160-170.
27 Cooper-Bishop, p.113; Lessons, p.112; Malovany, p.155; Woods et al Project 1946, pp.55-56 (herafter Project 1946); O'Ballance, pp. 60, 63-64; Pollack, p.195; Ward, pp.253-254; AISC, p. 5-17. For Operations 'Hoveyzeh'/'Nasr' see Volume 1, pp.45-46.
28 Malovany, p.155 & Volume 2, p. 17.
29 Malovany, pp.155-158; AISC, p.5.2.
30 Malovany, pp.168-170; AISC, p.5-2, Figure 5.1.
31 Lessons, pp. 126, 128; Malovany, pp. 173-174; O'Ballance, pp. 69, 78.
32 Malovany, pp. 128-129.
33 Malovany, pp.168, 171; AISC, pp. 5-4, Figures 5.2 & 5.3 & 5.4.
34 This chapter is largely based on Malovany, pp.282 & 790; DDB-1100-342-88 & DDB-2680-103-88.
35 Divisional strengths varied from 8,000 in 58th and 64th Infantry Divisions, to 25,000 in 21st Division, or from 10,000 in 88th Division to 18,000 in 81st Division. Most armoured brigades had fewer than 90 MBTs. The artillery groups usually totalled about 3,300 personnel and included 7 tube- and MRLS-battalions. IRIA's support formations included the Transportation- and Engineering Commands (the latter including engineering and bridging battalions), signal groups, and a supply framework based on the 1st and 2nd Area Support Commands (Kermanshah and Dezful, respectively).
36 The GMID identified the units in question as 7th Vali Asr, 9th Badr, 10th Seyed o-Shohada, 17th Ali Ibn Abu Talib, 19th Fajr, 21st Imam Reza, 27th Mohammad Rasoolallah, 31st Ashura, 32nd Ansar al-Hossein, 41st Sarallah, and 155th Seyed ol-Shohada Divisions. Some of units in question were actually 'borrowed' from the NFOHQ for the Operations Karbala-4/5/8. See CRRC SH-GMID-D-000-530.
37 SH-GMID-D-000-53
38 DDB-1100-342-88; DDB-2680-103-88 & DDB-1100-343-85, p.16.

39   The corps was scheduled to be designated VIII Corps but at Saddam's suggestion the unique command was renamed I Special Corps. It was disbanded in 1989.

40   SH-SHTP-D-000-538 & special thanks to General Makki for explaining the backgrounds.

41   SH-PDWN-D-000-730.

42   DDB-1100-343-85.

43   Malovany, p. 372.

44   Malovany, p.717; DDB-1100-343-85.

45   Malovany, pp.822-824; DDB-1100-342-88; DDB-2680-103-88.

46   The Iraqi term was (Qiyadet Jahafel al-Difa' al-Watani). Khoury, *Iraq in Wartime*, pp. 91-92, 99, 100-102, fn 40, 41, 43 (hereafter Khoury); Malovany, pp.827-828; Middle East Watch, *Genocide in Iraq*, Chapter 1 (herafter Watch with chapter number).

47   Khoury, p.101, p.101 fn 43 & Malovany, p.380 fn 2.

48   Ba'ath Regional Command Council, 01-2140-0003 quoted by Khoury, pp. 75 & 91-92.

49   Khoury, p.100 fn 37 & Watch, Chapter 1.

50   Bulloch & Morris, *The Gulf War*, p.253 (herafter Bulloch & Morris). NLA Chief of Staff Describes Operation 'Shining Sun', *NLA Quarterly*, Spring, 1988.

51   The fluent state of IRGC's formations during this period of war is readable in many of Iranian accounts, which variously describe the two Pasdaran-formations in the Task Force Nasr as brigades or divisions. The distinction appears to have been in their support elements.

52   For a photo of an Iranian mock-up of an Iraqi strongpoint, see DDB-1100-342-88, p. 21.

53   Buchan, Days of God p. 352 (hereafter Buchan); Cooper & Bishop, pp. 130-131; Farrokh, pp.363-364; Griffin article, p.21; Hiro, pp. 5556 &180; Lessons, pp. 128133, p. 144 fn 14, 17 & 18; Malovany, pp. 181-185; Murray & Woods, pp.175-177; O'Ballance, pp. 7882; Pelletiere, *The Iran-Iraq War*, p. 42 (hereafter Pelletiere); Pollack, *Arabs at War*, pp. 196-198 (hereafter Pollack); Ward, p. 256; Project 1946, pp. 74-76; AISC, pp. 6-1, 6-3, 6-7; DDB-1100-343-85, p. 66; Imposed War Official Web Site (http) sajed.ir; O'Ballance article, 'Iran vs Iraq: Quantity vs Quality?'.

54   Hiro, p. 55; Farrokh, p. 362; Project 1946, p. 75.

55   O'Ballance, p. 81.

56   Project 1946, p. 76.

57   Murray & Woods, p. 177; Pollack, p.196.

58   Farrokh, p. 364 (based upon J. Miller & L. Mylroie, *Saddam Hussein and the Crisis in the Gulf*, Times Books, New York, 1990, p. 114). General Makki recalls Saddam later related to this incident, too.

59   Pollack, p. 196 & O'Ballance, p. 29. Apparently, this was the first time the Basiji were deployed as conventional infantry on the battlefield. Until that time, they had been primarily used as labourers and porters.

60   Farrokh, p. 363.

61   O'Ballance, p. 82 & Buchan, p. 352.

62   See Volume 1, pp. 62-75.

63   Farrokh, p. 366; Lessons, p. 137; Malovany, pp. 185-186.

64   O'Ballance, pp. 8586; Lessons, p. 140; Malovany, pp. 198-216; AISC, pp. 6-10.

65   Connell, *Iranian Operation Decision-Making*, pp. 13-14 (hereafter Connell); Farrokh, p. 371; Malovany, pp. 216-219; O'Ballance, pp. 98-99; AISC, pp. 6-19 & 6-25.

66   'The Day of the Helicopter Gunship', *Baghdad Observer*, 27 October 1982. Widely accepted as 'truth' and repeated in multiple publications in the English language area of the 1980s, this claim was entirely unsubstantiated. Iraq never operated genuine Mi-24s (only the export variant Mi-25), and never received any AT-6s during the war with Iran. As far as is known 30 and more years later, no IrAAC Mi-25 has ever shot down any IRIAF F-4.

67   Connell, p. 14.

68   Ibid, pp. 14-16; Cooper & Bishop, pp. 144-145; Farrokh, p. 371-372; Hiro, p. 91; Lessons, p. 154; Malovany, pp. 221-224; O'Ballance,pp. 99101; AISC, pp. 6-25, 7-1, 7-6, Figures 6.18, 7.2.

69   AISC p. 6-25 & Cooper & Bishop, p. 147.

70   Why this operation not code-named Val Fajr-1 remains unknown, but its designation continues to confuse historians.

71   Hiro, p. 95; Farrokh, p. 373; Lessons, pp. 159-161; Malovany, pp. 225-228; O'Ballance, pp. 114-116; Ward, p. 261; AISC, pp. 7-1, 7-6, 7-7, Figure 7.2.

72   AISC, p. 7-7. US intelligence concluded the Iranians lost about 100 armoured fighting vehicles, including some 20 MBTs.

73   Marashi & Salama, pp. 135-136; Farrokh, p. 373; Lessons, p. 162; Malovany, pp. 228-230; O'Ballance, p. 118; AISC, p. 7.7; DDB-1100-343-85, pp. 67-68.

74   Cooper & Bishop, p. 156; Farrokh, pp. 374-375; Hiro, p. 97; Lessons, pp. 1678, 1703, 187 fn 17; Malovany, pp. 235-238; O'Ballance, pp. 119120; Ward, p. 261.

75   For Khaiber, see Volume 2, pp. 28-33. For Val Fajr-5 and -6, see Cooper & Bishop, p. 165; Cordesman, *The Iran-Iraq War and Western Security*, p. 62 (hereafter Cordesman); Farrokh, p. 377; Hiro, pp. 102-103; Lessons, p. 179; Malovany, p. 249; O'Ballance, pp. 142-143 & Ward, pp. 263-264.

76   Cooper & Bishop, p. 165; Farrokh, p. 377; Lessons, p. 179; Malovany, pp. 250-251; O'Ballance, p. 143 & Ward, pp. 263-264.

77   Cordesman, p. 69; Hiro, pp. 132-134; Malovany, pp. 264-265, O'Ballance, pp. 151-153.

78   The best sources for such tit-for-tat operations are Malovany, pp. 269-270 & 278-279, but also Farrokh, pp. 379-380; O'Ballance, p. 160 & DDB-1100-343-85, pp. 68-70 (Figure 27).

79   Malovany, pp. 315-316.

80   According to Makki: a senior member of Ba'th Party, Hamadi was appointed commander of 6th Armoured Division in 1988. He died in exile in Amman in 2013.

81   Marashi & Salama pp. 164 &190; Cooper & Bishop, pp. 215 & 217-219; Cordesman, pp. 101-103 & 118, fn 43; Farrokh pp. 389-390; Hiro, pp. 1712; Lessons, pp. 227228, 236, 264 fn 38; Malovany, pp. 317-319; O'Ballance, pp. 179180, 185, 189; Pelletiere, pp.103-104.

82   It remains unknown who took over as commander of 17th Armoured Division during the following period.

83   Malovany, p. 318.

84   Marashi & Salama, p. 190.

85   Malovany, pp. 326-327.

86   Pelletierre et al, Iraqi Power and US Security in the Middle East, pp. 15-16 (hereafter Iraqi Power).

87   Malovany, pp. 319 & 327.

88   Cordesman, p. 129; Hiro, p. 181; Lessons, pp. 256-257; Malovany, pp. 340-341; O'Ballance, p. 198 & SH-GMID-D-000-301, p. 26.

89   Cordesman, p. 260; Hiro, p. 185; O'Ballance, p. 203204

90   Malovany, pp. 345 & 358-359; SH-GMID-D-000-530. Malovany claims the latter attack was thwarted. However, in 1988, the Iraqis had to advance *towards* the river.

91   Cooper & Bishop, pp. 155-156, 222-223; Cordesman, pp. 137138; Farrokh, pp. 374 & 395-396; Hiro, pp. 967, 102, 174, 185; Lessons, pp. 166167, 187 fn 16, 234, 259, 266 fn 59 & 259260; Malovany, pp. 234-235, 282-285, 315-317, 343 & 356-357; Marashi & Salama, p. 142; O'Ballance, p. 119, 138139, 189 & 201; Pelletiere, pp. 76-77; Project 1946, pp. 90-95.

92   Iraqi Major-General Hamadani latter denied reports about deployment of chemical weapons during this campaign (see Project 1946). Helicopters of the IrAAF reportedly flew in 5,350 troops and 880 tons of supplies, while withdrawing 1,100 injured. Detail on Il-76s being deployed as bombers was provided by Brigadier-General Sadik (IrAF, ret.), in interview to Tom Cooper, March 2005.

93   Most of this chapter is based on Cordesman, pp. 98, 99, 111; Cooper & Bishop, pp. 157, 206; Farrokh, p. 375; Hiro, pp. 102, 169, 174, 185-186, 201; Lessons, pp. 161-162, 175177, 188 fn 23, 224225, 264 fn 26, 281-282, 292293, 362363 & 386-388; Malovany, pp. 238-243, 247 fn 9, 308-310, 354-357; Marashi & Salama, p. 170; O'Ballance, pp. 139140, 175, 180181; Pelletiere, pp. 76-78; Ward, p. 261 & Review of the Military Situation in Iraq by Colonel R.G.Eccles, *British Defence Attaché*, 27 April 1986.

94   Malovany, p. 242.

95   Interestingly, the Iraqi intelligence identified the presence of 23rd IRIA Special Forces Division and 1st Brigade of 64th IRIA Infantry Division on this sector in January 1988. This should have been reinforced by Pasdaran 9th Basdr Infantry Division, 39th Nabi al-Akram and 65th Kilan Rasht Infantry Brigdes, 622nd Beit-ol-Moghaddas Mountain-, 89th Moharram Artillery- and a mechanized brigade from 20th Ramadan Mechanized Division. SH-GMID-D-000-337.

96   For details on these three offensives, see Farrokh, p. 404; Hiro, p. 199; Malovany, pp. 367-368 & 430.

97   SH-PDWN-D-000-730.

98   Plagued by technical problems, this power station became operational again only in 2013.

99   For Tahrir ol-Quds see Cooper & Bishop, p. 165; Malovany, p. 249; O'Ballance, p. 141; Hiro, p. 149 & Lessons, p. 179.

100   During this attack, the Iraqis noted that the Pasdaran were now splitting their divisions into 'assault' and 'follow-up' elements, a concept first used by the Imperial Germany Army in 1918 (SH-GMID-D-000-530).

101   For Val Fajr-10, see Cooper & Bishop, pp. 262-263; Hiro, p. 202; Farrokh, p. 404; Lessons, pp. 369-372, 405406 fn 29; Malovany, pp. 370-373; Marashi & Salama, p. 172; Watch, Chapter 3; Project 1946, p. 83 & SH-GMID-D-000-530. In Project 1946 General Hamdani confusingly refers to these operations being in 1987. Watch also confuses Val Fajr-10, with Zafar-7 and Beit-al-Moghaddas-6.

102   Project 1946, pp. 83-84; Watch, Chapter 3; Nixon, *Debriefing the President*, pp. 122, 170-172 (hereafter Nixon) & Malovany, p. 371. While some Iraqis have claimed that this attack was an omen of the Anfal COIN campaign, there is strong evidence it was launched as a separate decision – one reflecting the massive use of chemical weapons in most Iraqi campaigns of 1988. Khazraji latter claimed that neither he nor any other military leader was involved, but that Saddam alone took the decision, in agreement with Majid and his military production chief – Hussein Kamel. On the contrary, Saddam denied all knowledge and blamed Khazraji. In Project 1946 General Hamdani claimed that Talbani had informed Baghdad that the Kurds, on his

instructions, had largely evacuated the area and optimistically claimed only '75-150' were killed. Most other Iraqi sources insist until today that either no chemical weapons were deployed by their armed forces against Halabja at all, or that this attack – or at least a part of it – was actually undertaken by the Iranians. For their part, the Iranians insist that Khomeini refused permission for development and deployment of chemical weapons because Islam prohibits those who fight for it from polluting the atmosphere – even in a 'Jihad' (Hiro, p201). The Iranian propaganda about the Halabja attack was designed to arouse public condemnation around the World – but had also the demoralising effects at home. Finally, there are notes that the Iraqi deployment of chemical weapons did play a part in their military success of 1988, but foremost as a part of 'superior tactics', rather than being the sole reason (Iraqi Power, p. 36).

103 Hiro, p. 202; Lessons, pp. 371-372 & Malovany, p. 373.
104 The Guards barely had time to unpack their kit bags before they were on the way back south to join the Faw offensive, apparently without the commando brigades, and to the bewilderment of the many Iraqi generals unaware of the planned offensive on Faw.
105 SH-GMID-D-000-530.
106 SH-SHTP-D-000-538.
107 Ibid.
108 Hiro, pp. 237-238 & 241; Lessons, p. 390; Malovany, pp. 425, 430-432.
109 For operations in 1981 see Lessons, pp. 97, 122 & O'Ballance, pp. 63-64, 133-134.
110 A. R., former Iranian Army NCO, interview by Tom Cooper, February 2004.
111 Hiro, p. 96; Lessons, p. 166 & O'Ballance, pp. 135-136 & 138-140.
112 Farrokh, p. 374.
113 As of late May 1983, the only Iraqi Army unit left in Kurdish-dominated parts of northern Iraq was 502nd Infantry Brigade, deployed in the BArzan-Zakho area (see SH-PDWN-D-000-730).
114 O'Ballance, p. 112 & Lortz, p. 55.
115 Farrokh, p. 374 & Watch, Chapter 1.
116 Hiro, pp. 59, 102, 141; Marashi & Salama, pp. 14 & 168; Lessons, p. 167; O'Ballance, pp. 135-138 & 141; Pelletiere, p. 78; Watch, Chapter 1 & DDB-1100-343-85.
117 According to Hiro (p. 149) this agreement had been signed in secrecy in 1978, but was made public only in 1984. It allowed each side to pursue 'subversive elements' up to 15 kilometres miles beyond the border.
118 Watch, Chapter 1.
119 Hiro, p. 149 & DDB-1100-343-85.
120 Cooper & Bishop, pp. 206 & 226; Cordsman, pp. 8283, 89, 98, 99, 111; Farrokh, p. 374; Hiro, pp. 150,169, 174; Lessons, pp. 200-201, 207208, 224-225, 257258, 264 fn 26 & 334-335 fn 27; Malovany, pp. 327-328; Marashi & Salama, p. 168; O'Ballance pp. 141, 167168, 175, 180-181; Watch, Chapter 1 & SH-MISC-D-001-3740.
121 Murray & Woods, p. 333.
122 Watch, Chapter 10, fn 5 & Lortz, p. 40.
123 Watch, Chapter 1 & Project 1946, pp. 94-95.
124 Ibid.
125 'Kirkuk oilfield raid-damage disputed', *Jane's Defence Weekly*, 18 October 1987.
126 In a broadcast on 13 June 1988 the unnamed commander of the 'Ramadan' headquarters claimed that in addition to major offensives the previous 12 months saw 496 minor operations which claimed to have destroyed or captured 170 AFVs, 1,525 soft-skinned vehicles, 87 guns and to have captured 50,000 individual and crew-served weapons. Foreign Broadcast Information Services/British Library.
127 Hiro, pp. 185-86 & 191; Lessons, pp. 257, 259, 292, 319320, 3701, 405 fn 27; Malovany, pp. 354-357; O'Ballance, pp. 200-201; 'Kurdish villages razed in punitive Iraqi campaign', *Jane's Defence Weekly*, 10 October 1987; Foreign Broadcast Information Services/British Library & SH-MISC-D-001-3740.
128 Sadik, interview, March 2005.
129 Khoury, p.100 fn 43.
130 Malovany, pp.822-824.
131 Lessons, pp. 320 & 370-371; Watch, Chapter 1 & SH-GMID-D-000-530.
132 Watch (Chaper 1) reports deployment of guns with 25 miles (40 kilometres) range. Given the Soviet-made M-46s have had a range of 27 kilometres, it is possible that the Iraqis deployed some Austrian-made GHN-45 155mm guns.
133 Watch, Chapters 1 & 2.
134 SH-MISC-D-001-3740; Hiro, p. 197; Marashi & Salama, p. 170; Murray & Woods, pp. 253, 310-311; Watch, Chapter 39. Majid should have personally executed up to 30 prisoners in Basra, in 1991.
135 Murray & Woods, p. 332. The NDBs were reportedly concentrated into five divisional-sized commands (see Malovany, p. 828).
136 Lessons, p. 288; Murray & Woods, pp. 254-255, 311, 332-334; O'Ballance, p. 149 & SH-SHTP-A-001-045.
137 See Air 19/109 Method of Employment of the Air Arm in Iraq 1924. The commander of No 45 Squadron in Iraq during this period was Squadron Leader Arthur Harris, the wartime commander of Bomber Command and an advocate of area attack (and also known as 'Bomber Harris').
138 Watch, Chapter 2.
139 Ibid.
140 For operations in 1988 see Lessons, p. 383; Malovany, pp. 357, 370-371; Watch, Chapter 2; Foreign Broadcast Information Services/British Library & SH-MISC-D-001-3740.
141 Murray & Woods, pp. 332-334 quoting SH-SHTP-A-000-788.
142 Marashi & Salama, p. 172; Malovany, pp. 368-373 & 440-442; Murray & Woods, pp. 333-334; Khazraji, *Al Harb Al Iraqiya*, pp. 581-598 (hereafter Khazraji); Khoury, pp. 33, 118-121, 216; Watch, Chapters 3-7 & 10; CHAK web site & Military Campaign, pp. 17-41.
143 Malovany, p. 372.
144 CHAK (p. 23) identifies 37 brigades including four commando/Special Forces but this seems unlikely.
145 Watch, Chapter 11.
146 For the aftermath of the offensives see Watch, Chapter 12 & CHAK web site (pp. 5 & 75).
147 SH-PDWN-D-000-730.
148 SH-SHTP-D-000-538.
149 Farrokh, pp. 411-412; Hiro, p. 238; Lessons, p. 395; Khazraji, pp. 537-561; Makki, *Maarik at-Tahrir al-Kubra al-Iraqiya*, pp. 383-402 (hereafter Makki); Malovany, pp. 425-440, 448 fn 1, 449 fn 3; Pelletiere, p. 144; Iraqi Power, p. 30; Pollack, p. 228 & Ward, p. 295.
150 Lessons, pp. 395396.
151 Hiro, p. 246; Iraqi Power, pp. 30-31; Lessons, pp. 387 & 396398; Khazraji, pp. 561-580; Makki, pp. 403-462; Malovaney, pp. 432-438, 440; Pelletiere, pp. 144-145; Pollack, pp. 227-228; 'Iraq's southern successes', *Jane's Defence Weekly*, 23 July 1988. For III Corps' contribution see Volume 3.
152 See Volume 3 and Malovany, pp. 438-439.
153 For the background to MeK/MKO's activities see Hiro, pp. 69 99-101, 202, 230-231 & O'Ballance, pp. 89-90.
154 Bulloch & Morris, p. 235.
155 Ibid, pp. 254-255.
156 Buchan, pp. 370-371; Bulloch & Morris, pp. 252-257; Hiro, p. 202; Lessons, pp. 320-321; Malovany, pp. 356 & 377; 'Mujahideen strength growing in Iran', *Jane's Defence Weekly*, 28 December 1986; 'NLA and the struggle against Tehran', *Jane's Defence Weekly*, 20 February 1988; 'Operation 'Shining Sun', *NLA Quarterly*, Spring 1988 & 'Special Report', *NLA Quarterly*, Autumn 1988.
157 Farrokh, p. 410; Hiro, p. 209; Lessons, pp. 387388, 408 fn 73 & 75; Pollack, p. 227; 'Iraq in successful attack on occupied territory', *Jane's Defence Weekly*, 2 July 1988 & 'Disarming Khomeinei', *Special Report*, NLA Quarterly, Autumn 1988.
158 Final Report on Operation Eternal Light, General Command of the National Liberation Army; Bulloch & Morris, pp. 255-257; Farrokh, pp. 413-414; Hiro, pp. 246247; Lessons, pp. 398, 409 fn 103; Malovany, pp. 439 & website <iran-e-azad.org/English>
159 Bulloch & Morris, p.253.